Marie Lechler

An econometrical analysis of the interdependencies between the demographic transition and democracy

Anchor Academic
Publishing

Lechler, Marie: An econometrical analysis of the interdependencies between the demographic transition and democracy. Hamburg, Anchor Academic Publishing 2014

Buch-ISBN: 978-3-95489-258-7
PDF-eBook-ISBN: 978-3-95489-758-2
Druck/Herstellung: Anchor Academic Publishing, Hamburg, 2014

Bibliografische Information der Deutschen Nationalbibliothek:
Die Deutsche Nationalbibliothek verzeichnet diese Publikation in der Deutschen Nationalbibliografie; detaillierte bibliografische Daten sind im Internet über http://dnb.d-nb.de abrufbar.

Bibliographical Information of the German National Library:
The German National Library lists this publication in the German National Bibliography. Detailed bibliographic data can be found at: http://dnb.d-nb.de

Hermannstal 119k, 22119 Hamburg
http://www.diplomica-verlag.de, Hamburg 2014
Printed in Germany

Abstract

This paper investigates the effect of an exogenous demographic transition on democracy. As possible channels through which this influence makes an impact, education and per capita income and, to a lesser degree, urbanization were identified. These interdependencies were tested using pooled ordinary least squares as well as fixed effects models on the basis of panel data. In conclusion, the demographic transition affects democracy through the aforementioned channels primarily in poor countries that have experienced their demographic transition and subsequent democratization in the second half of the 20th century or later.

Table of contents

List of figures

List of tables

List of Abbreviations

FE: Fixed effects

GDP: Gross domestic product

HAC: Heteroskedasticity-and autocorrelation- consistent

HR: Heteroskedasticity-robust

iid: independent and identically distributed

OLS: Ordinary Least Squares

OVB: Omitted variable bias

WDI: World Development Indicators

3SLS: Three Stage Least Squares

1. Introduction

"[...] in many ways demographic change can and should be seen as an essential factor of change that has profound implications for society" (Reher, 2011, p.12).

The demographic transition[1] has been part of a global transition process that involved changes in politics, economics and society in almost every country. These different processes all have partially overlapping causes and consequences. Therefore, it seems obvious that these movements of change are all interrelated, which is supported by an abundance of research on causal relationships between economic growth and democracy as well as between economic growth and the demographic transition. However, only few works focus on interdependencies between the demographic transition and democratization, even though these two processes happened roughly at the same time and are therefore likely to influence each other. Thus, the goal of this paper is to analyze the relationship between the demographic transition and democracy and the possible channels through which their influences take effect[2].

First of all, the direction of causality has to be identified in this context. Dyson (2010) and Reher (2011) classify the onset of mortality decline, which constitutes the starting point of the demographic transition as an exogenous event. One might argue that the demographic transition is linked to a country's health level, which in turn depends on a country's political system because only in democratic countries medicine is distributed equally and investments in health are undertaken. While this holds true in a not globalized world, in modern times basic health care is provided through the international community. Hence, differences in the standard of health care caused by the respective political systems are not large enough to cause a demographic transition. Therefore, the direction of causation from democracy to demography can be neglected.

Democratization very much depends on factors such as education, income, urbanization and women's empowerment, which can be identified as consequences of the demographic transition. Hence, the dominant direction of causation seems to go from demography to democracy. The demographic transition brings about the effect on these factors in the following way:

[1] Characterized as transition from high mortality and fertility rates to low mortality and fertility rates. Declining mortality rates (and thereby rising life expectancies) followed by falling fertility rates, eventually, lead to a higher proportion of old people in society.

[2] holding income constant

Higher life expectancies and fewer children per family increase investments in education and thereby raise a country's educational level. Due to changing age structures and better health conditions, more people are part of a country's labor force increasing its productivity and eventually resulting in economic growth. Fewer children also support women's empowerment since women have more personal free time besides caring for the household and can participate in the labor force as well. Finally, changing age structures and higher life expectancies also lead to urbanization: more people move to cities due to better employment opportunities and improvements in the health level, which affect mortality rates in cities more than in rural areas because in cities the danger of infectious diseases is much higher.
Furthermore, education, income, women's empowerment and urbanization affect democracy, which is established in most major works on democracy, as for example by Lipset (1959), Huntington (1991) and Barro (1999).
Hence, it is likely that an exogenous demographic transition causes better education, higher income, women's empowerment and urbanization, which in turn leads to democracy.

An empirical analysis therefore tests the hypotheses whether the demographic transition has a statistically significant influence on democracy and, if that is the case, through which channels this influence takes effect. For this purpose, panel data from more than 150 countries since 1800 are examined using different linear pooled ordinary least squares and linear fixed effect models. In addition, interactions with income are tested and a channel analysis is executed. In order to ensure the exogeneity of the demographic transition suitable control variables, most importantly per capita income, are included.

Quantifying these effects is important because an advanced understanding of the determinants of democracy facilitates more profound forecasts for democratization movements all over the world and provides guidelines to influence these processes as policy maker. This is highly relevant since many political instable African and Asian countries, such as Congo, Somalia, Afghanistan and Yemen, are currently undergoing the demographic transition or have just completed this process.

The paper is organized as follows: the topic is introduced by first explaining the motivating theory by giving an overview of the literature concerning the demographic transition and determinants of democracy and by demonstrating the connection between these two subjects. Based on the theoretical part the econometrical analysis subsequently follows and finally leads to a conclusion about the stated hypotheses.

2. Motivating Theory

Many authors argue that the demographic transition is part of a global transition process not only involving demographic but also social, economic and political changes[3]. This temporal parallelism of change processes in economics, politics, demography and on the social level gives rise to the assumption that they are all interrelated.

While the focus of previous research lay mainly on the relationships between economics and democracy[4] or demography and economics[5] this paper focuses on the interdependencies between the demographic transition and democratization processes. For this purpose the consequences of the demographic transition and determinants of democracy are analyzed.

2.1. The demographic transition

Thompson already assumed in 1929 that certain historical stages of nations are linked to their regarding mortality and fertility rates. Notestein (1945) then developed a more detailed four-stage model based on observations in the Western World. His findings demonstrate that mortality rates start to decline at one point in the history of a country while fertility rates remain high, which leads to population growth. With a delay, however, fertility rates start to decline as well and once mortality and fertility rates both reach a low steady state the population stops growing. An illustration of this process according to Sunde&Cervelatti[6] (2011, p. 103) is presented in figure 1. MT denotes the onset of the mortality transition, which is succeeded by population growth. With a time delay fertility rates start to decline as well (FT) and thus population growth slows down. This process is called "demographic transition", which is defined in this paper by two criterions that have to be fulfilled by a country in order to be classified as post-transitional[7]: the life expectancy has to be above fifty and crude birthrates[8] below thirty. These criterions are two out of three used by Sunde&Cervelatti (2011, p.107) in accordance with Chesnais' (1992, p.19) norms. The third one, a sustained decline in fertility, is hard to quantify and left out because the

---

3 See, for example, Dyson (2010) or Reher (2011)

4 Barro (1996), Glaeser et al. (2004), Acemoglu et al. (2008),

5 Bloom,Canning&Sevilla (2001), Reher (2011), Lorentzen,McMillan&Wacziarg (2005), Acemoglu&Johnson (2006), Cervelatti&Sunde(2011)

6 The figure reproduces Fig. 1.1 from Chesnais (1992) and Fig. 4.2 from Livi-Bacci (1992).

7 Post-transitional: Countries that experienced the onset of the demographic transition

8 Crude birth rates denote the number of births per 1000 people per year

criterion of crude birth rates below thirty is more restrictive and therefore ensures the satisfaction of the third criterion as well.

Another definition of demographic transition is given by Reher (2004, p.21), who identifies the starting point as "the beginning of the first quinquennium after a peak, where fertility declines by at least 8% over two quinquennia and never increases again to levels approximating the original take-off point" (Reher, 2004, p.21). The dates of the demographic transition computed by employing above mentioned criterions as well as Reher's specification are presented in appendix B.1.

Thus, a pre-transitional society with high mortality and fertility rates is rather young compared to a post-transitional society that is characterized by higher life expectancies and lower fertility rates. A society's changing age structure is considered as one of the most important features of the demographic transition (Reher, 2011, p.14).

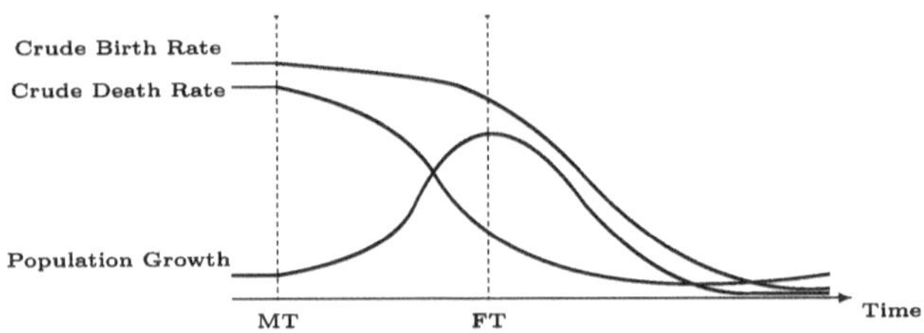

Figure 1 The demographic transition

Empirical studies confirm that a general pattern of an antecedent mortality decline and a following fertility decline exists, even though the time lag between these two developments differs across countries[9]. Reher (2004), for example, observed this demographic process in most countries in the past 150 years and categorizes countries according to the date of their demographic transition, whereby he identifies four groups. The first group constitutes the "forerunners", whose fertility decline started before 1935 and which are mainly European and a few American countries. The so-called "followers" are countries that experienced their fertility decline between 1950 and 1964 and are either somehow influenced by the Europeans, via power regimes or ethnicity, or countries that are distinguished because of their special regional position such as India, Singapore and Japan. The fertility decline of the third group took place between 1965 and 1979 and therefore, this group is labeled "trailers", which includes the rest of Latin America and some African and Asian countries. The last group is referred to as the "latecomers", whose demographic transition started only after 1980 and which consists of some Asian and

[9] See for example Coale (1975)

most of the African countries[10]. It is important to note that the general pattern of the demographic transition has been the same in all countries - only the time of the onset and the duration of the transition differ.

There is, however, no consensus about possible causes of the mortality decline because it occurred worldwide under different circumstances and, thus, no one has succeeded in establishing a general pattern, which could be employed to explain the occurrence of the demographic transition in all countries yet. Therefore, some authors, such as Dyson (2010) and Reher (2011)[11], claim that the demographic transition occurs exogenously.

As opposed to this exogeneity assumption, one might argue that health care (and thereby the occurrence of a demographic transition) is linked to a country's income and its political system. That is, because only rich nations can afford medicine and only democratic nations have an interest in distributing it, which would mean that the onset of the demographic transition depends on a country's political and economic situation[12]. Globalization, however, raised awareness for the health situation worldwide and international organizations as well as foreign governments have started to provide basic health care for people in less developed countries. Furthermore, globalization facilitates the adoption of new medical inventions and progress in research so that even poor countries can benefit from the latest scientific achievements. This means that in a globalized world a country's income and political system are not strong enough to cause a demographic transition.

Thus, the argument that income or the political system have a significant effect on the demographic transition might be valid for the 18th and 19th century- in modern times, however, national income and democracy levels only play a minor role in determining a country's health situation[13].

Besides from income and the political system as the main threats to the exogeneity assumption of the demographic transition, other factors such as education, women's empowerment and

[10] See appendix B.1 for a summary of the Reher-groups

[11] Canning (2011,p.3): "tackling the central thesis of the book [Dyson's Population and development, 2010] which is that the demographic transition is a largely self-contained process that proceeds independently of social and economic development. The argument is that the mortality transition occurs exogenously and is the cause of a subsequent decline in fertility "

Reher (2004,p. 12): The demographic transition "is considered as a largely autonomous process".

[12] Franco et al. (2004) and Cutler et al. (2006), for example, argue that political institutions significantly affect health and Pritchett &Summers (1996) state that income has a significant effect on health.

[13] Smith (2003) and Adams et al. (2003) find that changes in income and lagged values of income do not predict changes in health.

Christopher Martyn questions the strength of the evidence for politics being a determinant of health in Franco's paper (2004) (p.1423)

urbanization might still be correlated with the occurrence of the demographic transition. Therefore, the empirical models account for these factors. Hence following analyses consider the demographic transition as a predominantly exogenous event.

2.2. Democracy

There exist a variety of definitions of democracy and the most common ones in recent literature are based on Schumpeter's (1947) characterization[14], such as, for example, Huntington's (1991,p.6) description: "The central procedure of democracy is the selection of leaders through competitive elections by the people they govern". He points out the significance of a free and fair election process in order to show the importance of a high participation rate to achieve a "people's rule"[15].

Lipset (1959), in accordance with Schumpeter (1947) and Weber (1946), defines three conditions that classify a democracy: Firstly, a "political formula", which is a value system that legitimizes the system, specifies institutions and is accepted by all citizens, is necessary. Secondly, one set of political leaders in office is as important as, thirdly, several sets of political leaders out of office that form an opposition. Furthermore, "opportunities for changing governing officials" (p.71) have to be allowed and the "largest possible part of the population" (p.71) has to be able to influence political decisions. He thereby underlines not only the necessity of a balanced distribution of power to avoid conflicts and autocratic movements, but also the necessity of equal and free participation opportunities for the citizens.

The concepts of freedom along with equality among all citizens appear in most work about democracy and are therefore the underlying definition applied in this paper. The criterions to quantify this definition are discussed in the empirical part.

In 2011, 87 countries, representing 43 percent of the global population, are considered democracies, while 48 countries, representing 35 percent of the world's population, are classified as "not free" according to Freedom House[16]. The degree of freedom and democratization in the

---

[14] "The democratic method is that institutional arrangement for arriving at political decisions in which individuals acquire the power to decide by means of a competitive struggle for the people's vote" (as cited in Barro, 1999, p. 160).

[15] "Democracy" comes from the Greek words δῆμος (*dēmos*) meaning "people" and κράτος (*kratos*) meaning "power"

[16] The number of countries qualifying as partly free stood at 60 and they were home to 22 percent of the world's total population (http://www.freedomhouse.org/report/freedom-world-2012/full-report-essay). Freedom House is a US-based non-governmental organization that supports democratic change, monitors freedom, and advocates democracy and human rights around the world.

world is higher than ever before in history. But still, more than half of the world's population lives in unfree or only partially free countries. Questions regarding reasons for democratization movements are often raised in this context, for example: which factors determine democracy and the different timing of democratization processes?

The temporally different occurrence of democratizations is examined most famously by Samuel Huntington, who identifies three different democratization waves[17], each succeeded by reverse movements. The first wave had its origins in the American and French revolution and took place during the relatively long period between 1828 and 1926 mainly in Europe, but also in North America and in a few Latin American countries. The second one occurred after World War II, when Allied occupation promoted democratization processes, most of Latin America democratized and the end of Western colonial rule produced new states, some of which became democratic as well. The third wave started in 1974 and includes many democratization processes in Latin America and South and Eastern Europe after the collapse of the Soviet Union (Huntington, 1993, p.13 f.)[18].

An abundance of authors addressed the question about causes for democratizations and detected determinants reaching from economic to historical and social factors. Most major works on democratization- except Acemoglu et al. (2008)- agree that economic factors are favorable for democracies. They, however, have not reached a consensus concerning the exact pattern of these effects[19].

Other discussed determinants of democracy include education, health, social institutions, religion, historic factors (such as, for example, a colonial history), urbanization, ethnologic fragmentation and geography[20]. Analyzing all these factors would go beyond the scope of this paper, and therefore the focus in following sections lies on factors that are at the same time considered as possible consequences of the demographic transition.

---

17 "A wave of democratization is a group of transitions from nondemocratic to democratic regimes that occur within a specified period of time and that significantly outnumber transitions in the opposite direction during that period of time"(Huntington, 1993, 15)

18 See appendix B.2 for a summary of countries belonging to the different democratization-waves

19 See Lipset (1959), Huntington (1991), Rusechemeyer,Stephens&Stephens (1992) or Barro (1999)

20 Lipset (1959), Huntington (1991), Barro (1999), Papaioannou and Siourounis (2006), Glaeser et al. (2007), Hegre et al. (2012)

2.3. Interdependencies between the demographic transition and democracy

Since the demographic transition and democratization processes often happened roughly at the same time, it is surprising that only a limited amount of literature focuses on the political consequences of demographic transitions while many authors examine the effects on the economy and on society.

As explained in section 2.1, the occurrence of a demographic transition is, in modern times, largely independent from the political system. Thus, the following section analyzes reasons and possible channels through which demography influences democracy. While the reverse direction of causation cannot be ruled out completely, the causation from the demographic transition to democracy is considered as the dominant direction.

As one of the few authors who addresses the political implications of a demographic transition, Dyson (2010) points out the higher confidence people have in their future after the demographic transition and the resulting increased awareness for political matters. "The rise in the number of years that they could reasonably expect to live, surely had an influence in helping people to think more about issues of justice and political equity" (p. 202). Moreover, he emphasizes certain outcomes of the transition such as urbanization and population ageing that eventually lead to democratization.

Another approach was developed by Cincotta (2007), who argues that political systems in pre-transitional, young societies are more likely to be instable than in post-transitional societies. This youth bulge argument, derived from civil conflict research[21], is connected with the logic of authoritarian bargains[22] in order to explain the occurrence of authoritarian regimes in pre-transitional societies. That is, before the demographic transition political instability is more likely to occur due to the young age structure of society and because of this insecure environment people are willing to exchange political rights for security. Hence, democracy is less likely to arise in pre-transitional than in older, post-transitional societies. This argumentation is based on the assumption that if people do not have a reason (in this case higher levels of security) to call for an authoritarian regime the chances for democracy increase. Cincotta's approach, therefore, rather focuses on the determinants of authoritarian regimes than on the determinants of democracy.

---

[21] See Goldstone (1991, 2001) and Collier (2000) for theoretical explenantion and Urdal (2006) for empirical evidence

[22] "The social contract in dictatorships is commonly explained as an "authoritarian baragain" between rulers and citizens by which citizens relinquish political rights for economic security" (Desai, Olofsgard, Yusuf, 2009, Abstract)

This paper, however, focuses on the direct effects of the demographic transition and its consequences on democracy and consequently follows Dyson's approach (2010). It is likely that longer time horizons and more life experience promote democracy because people have a broader array of perspectives and are able to evaluate a political system more critically. In addition, the longer people expect to live and work in a society the more they want to participate in the political system that sets the general framework for how society works. Furthermore, more life experience also makes people more familiar with different political systems and the respective advantages and disadvantages. Thus, a movement towards democracy is more probable in societies with higher life expectancies than in others.

Besides from the effect of higher life expectancies on democracy, consequences of the demographic transition such as education, urbanization, women's empowerment and economic growth also play an important role since they are at the same time determinants of democracy. There might also be other factors that connect the demographic transition and democracy. The aforementioned ones, however, seem to be the most significant ones and therefore the focus in the following course of this paper will lay on these four.
In order to deduce these relationships, the subsequent sections explain these factors with respect to the effect the demographic transition has on each one of them and the influence of these factors on democracy.

2.3.1. Education

Lower fertility rates and higher life expectancies do not only change the structure of society as a whole, but also family structures. Fewer children per family increase the share of disposable income for each child's education and higher life expectancies increase the return on investments in education. Declining mortality rates also increase the incentive for societal investments in education because society benefits from an educated labor force for a longer time period. Bar and Leukhina (2011) argue that lower mortality rates lead to better knowledge transmission because individuals are carriers of ideas, which also contributes to a higher level of education in post-transitional societies than in others. Empirical studies support the positive relationship between the demographic transition and education as well (e.g. Lorentzen, 2005).

The second part of the argument - the influence of education on democracy - is a rather old field of study. John Dewey argued in favor of education to obtain democracy as early as 1916 because in educated societies people understand political contexts better, are encouraged to think about different forms of governance and question critically the current political situation. In the past fifteen years, however, a passionate debate about the empirical evidence for this relationship has arisen. Barro (1999), for example, states in his study about the origins of democracy that the propensity for democracy rises with years of schooling. Even though Acemoglu (2005) criticizes Barro's and other's studies for using wrong models[23] and, in his analysis, finds no evidence for a link between education and democracy, many other authors succeeding him, who use revised and more sophisticated models such as Glaeser et. al (2006), Papaioanou et al. (2008),Wacziarg (2011) and Hegre el. al (2012), support the idea of a causal relationship between education and democracy theoretically as well as empirically.

Hence, democracy is very likely to occur in more educated societies. After a demographic transition people invest more in education, a better knowledge transfer takes place and more people have more time to study so that better education is a direct result of this transition and thereby is one element that connects the demographic transition and democracy.

2.3.2. Urbanization

"Any account of the demographic transition that fails to include urbanization as one of its major components is seriously incomplete" (Dyson, 2011). Studies on urbanization often refer to economic changes to explain a drift towards cities. Mortality rates and population growth, however, are an important determinant of urbanization as well. Therefore, de Vries (1990) developed the „stylized sector-specific model of the demographic transition" and its implications for urban growth. In pre-transitional times, death rates in urban areas are usually higher than in rural areas because infectious diseases, communicated by contagion in confined space, were the main cause for high mortality rates. The demographic transition then reduced mortality rates through better health care, with the result that the urban mortality rate fall more rapidly than the rural mortality rate. Thus, the urban population increased faster than the rural population as long as the birthrate was higher than the death rate. Once birth and death rates reached the same level, the process of the demographic transition was completed and the result was an increase of the urban population. Another connection between the demographic transition and urbanization is a temporary strong population growth in general, which does not only contribute to relative faster growth of cities compared to rural areas but also to new city foundings, resulting in absolute urban growth. Empirical evidence for the relationship between the demographic transition and urbanization is given by Woods (2003). In addition, Dyson (2010, 2011) and Canning (2011) establish a similar argumentation and agree that mortality decline increased the urban population.

[23] According to Acemoglu country and time fixed effects are crucial for regressions that estimate the effect of education on democracy.

Urbanization as a determinant of democracy is extensively discussed since "democracy made its first effective appearance in the Greek city states" (Laski, 1937, p. 76). Max Weber (1950, p. 315) characterizes cities as a certain type of political community, which is confirmed by Lipset's analysis about the requisites of democracy (1960)[24]. One of the main arguments in this discussion is that people in cities can organize themselves more easily and have a better notion of inequalities and the political situation, which promotes exercising political rights and democratic movements. Moreover, cities are characterized by a growing middle class[25], which is often identified as an important component of democracy (Lipset, 1959).

Dyson (2010) emphasizes the different distribution of political power in cities, which is promoted through new administrative and governance structures that become necessary in urban areas. But he also argues that democracy can only arise in moderate growing cities because cities growing too quickly, which have to deal with space problems, involve the danger of civil conflict and political unrest.

Barro (1999), on the other hand, claims that according to his empirical studies democracy tends to fall in line with urbanization, but does not give a profound theoretical explanation for this negative relationship. Therefore, these results could have either occurred due to theoretical explanations, which have not been covered so far[26] or due to estimation errors. Since the majority of authors, however, argue in favor of a positive relationship between urbanization and democratization this paper follows this approach.

Urban governance structures, a broader middle class and better communication facilities than in rural areas all have a positive effect on democratization. Thus, urbanization can be seen as another outcome of the demographic transition that causes democratization.

2.3.3. Women's empowerment

Declining fertility rates have a huge impact on women's lives because caring for fewer children gives them more time to spend, for example, at school or at work. Being more educated and pursuing a profession also goes along with becoming independent, self-confident and accepting social and political responsibilities. There are many empirical studies that find a large negative effect of a high fertility rate on female labor force participation (Bloom, Canning, Fink, Finlay, 2009) and on female economic and political empowerment (Canning, 2010). Dyson (2001, 2010)

[24] See also Mumford (1995, p.21) and Amin & Thrift (2004, p. 231) and their argumentation in favor of a positive correlation between cities and democracy

[25] The middle class grows in cities extraordinary fast due to the economic structure of cities (new type of occupations are available)

[26] For example that autocratic regimes can control cities easier than other areas

also claims that fertility and mortality declines lead to a reduction in gender differentiation and higher female autonomy.

Women's empowerment contributes to democratization because equality and broad participation are its prerequisites. Barro (1999) agrees with this position by stating that "democracy is also negatively and significantly related to the gap between male and female primary attainment", meaning that higher levels of democracy can be reached in more equal societies. Waylan (1996) emphasizes the substantial role of women in bringing about the collapse of authoritarianism in Latin America and Eastern Europe.
Consequently, the demographic transition, particularly fertility decline, promotes women's empowerment, which in light of higher equality among the citizens determines democracy.

2.3.4. Economic growth

There are several arguments in favor of a positive influence of the demographic transition on economic growth. Higher life expectancies and more people in an employable age increase the labor force, and it becomes more productive through higher health levels (Bloom, Canning, Sevilla, 2001). Lorentzen et al. (2005) argue that high pre-transitional mortality rates reduce economic growth because they shorten time horizons and lead to risky behavior and lower investments in physical and human capital. They also see mortality rates as a source of the poverty trap because poor health conditions and a weak economy reinforce each other. Hence, post-transitional societies are characterized by better prerequisites for economic growth. Not only Galor and his Unified Growth Theory (2011), but also Canning (2011), in accordance with Dyson (2010) and Dahan & Tsiddon (1998) suggests that the demographic transition played a major role in the emergence of economic growth, primarily because of mortality decline and age-structural changes. This relationship was questioned by Acemoglu & Johnson (2006), who do not obtain evidence that large increases in life expectancy lead to increases in per capita income. Sunde&Cervelatti (2011), however, find in post-transitional times a positive relationship of life expectancy on economic growth, even though the effect before the demographic transition is ambiguous. Hence, according to the overwhelming majority of literature, economic growth is at least partially determined by the demographic transition.

The tendency that richer countries are often more democratic can be observed worldwide. If there is a direct connection between income and democracy is, however, controversial. While Acemoglu et al. (2008) did not find evidence for a causal relationship in empirical studies, Barro (1999), for example, did. Most major works on democracy (Lipset,1959, Huntington 1991,

Rueschmeyer/Stephens/Stephens, 1992, Tavres/Wacziarg, 2000, Murtin/Wacziarg, 2011) consider economic performance as a determinant – perhaps even the main one. They argue that wealth is a prerequisite for intelligent participation in political processes since people have the ability to think about broader questions, such as governance systems, as they are usually better educated. It also changes the social position of workers and strengthens the middle class, which has a positive impact on civic participation. Economic growth also weakens the power of a small economically and therefore often politically leading class and raises the influence of the working class.

Hence, the demographic transition promotes economic growth, which is a determinant of democracy so that income is, besides education, urbanization and women's empowerment, a fourth channel through which demographic transition and democracy are connected.

Accordingly, this analysis yields two hypotheses, which will be examined in the empirical part of this paper

(1.) The demographic transition has a positive influence on the rise of democracy.

(2.) The effect of the demographic transition on democracy works primarily through the channels of education, women's empowerment, urbanization and economic growth.

3. Data and descriptive statistics

3.1. Data

In order to support these hypotheses the following section provides an empirical analysis based on different linear panel data models for more than 150 countries over the past 200 years. Panal data are advantageous compared to cross-sectional or time-series data because they „usually give the resarcher a large number of data points, increasing the degrees of freedom and reducing the collinearity among explanatory variables-hence improving the efficiency of econometric estimates“ (Hsiao, 2003, p.3). Moreover, panel data are particularly useful to analyze the dynamics of change regarding demography and democracy across different countries. There are, however, also limitations of using panel data, such as sample selection bias because data availability might not be equal across countries and years.

Demographic data, such as life expectancy and fertility rates, were taken from the World Bank's world development indicator database (WDI) and are available since 1960. This database also contains statistics on education, urbanization, female labor force participation and GDP. GDP and other economic variables were also drawn from Acemoglu&Johnson (2007) and Banks' cross national time series database[27]. As another measure of education, the Barro-Lee dataset of educational attainment in the world is used, which provides data about average years of schooling in 5-year intervals from 1950 until 2010. As measure for democratization, Polity IV data[28] as "the most widely used data resource for studying regime change and the effects of regime authority“[29] are employed, which cover the time span from 1800 to 2010 for more than 150 countries. A detailed description of all variables and sources is given in appendix A.

3.1.1. Demographic data

The most important demographic data are mortality and fertility rates in order to estimate the date of the demographic transition. As one measure, a binary variable labeled demographic transition ("demotran") was created, which turns 1 if life expectancy is higher than fifty and crude birthrates fall below 30/1000. If one of these criterions is not met the variable stays 0. Life

[27] This database was launched by Arthur Banks in 1968 at the State University of New York at Binghampton and provides data for more than 200 countries from 1815 until 2007 (Arthur S. Banks, "Cross-National Time-Series Data Archive (CNTS) 1815-2007", http://hdl.handle.net/1902.1/11448 Databanks International [Distributor] V1 [Version])

[28] The Polity IV Project is is under the direction of Dr. Monty G. Marshall and supported by the Political Instability Task Force, Societal-Systems Research, and Center for Systemic Peace.

[29] http://www.systemicpeace.org/polity/polity4.htm

expectancy as taken from the World Bank dataset is defined as "number of years a newborn infant would live if prevailing patterns of mortality at the time of its birth were to stay the same throughout its life"[30] and crude birth reflect the number of live births occurring during the year, per 1,000 population and are estimated at midyear. As the World Bank data are only available since 1960, all analyses including the binary variable "demotran" only take into account countries that experienced their transition after 1960.

Data about the onset of fertility decline from Reher's analysis (2004)[31] are taken as another measure for the demographic transition.

The difference between these two measures amounts to 15 years on average with a standard deviation of 10.3, which is due to the fact that Reher's data underlies a different definition for the demographic transition than the one applied for the World Bank data. Also, the data of the World Bank only start in 1960 while Reher's data go back to 1900. Thus, only data for countries that experienced their demographic transition after 1960 can be compared, which are mainly African, Asian and some Latin American countries (whose data are less accurate). Taking this into consideration, the two measures from completely different datasets are quite close in terms of the time horizon they reflect.

In addition, the time difference between the present and the time of the demographic transition (yearssincedt)[32] were calculated on the basis of Reher's data. For summary statistics of the demographic data see appendix C.

In the following course of the analysis WDI data underlie the binary variable "demotran" and Reher's data are the basis for the continuous variable "years passed since (pending to) the demographic transition". It is important to keep in mind that the variables reflect different time horizons[33] and different meanings. While the binary variable "demotran" measures the effect of the occurrence of the demographic transition (in the past) on democracy today, the continuous variable represents the effect that years passed since or pending to the demographic transition have on democracy today. Thus, the results from these different strategies to examine the stated hypotheses have to be interpreted with respect to their respective time horizon and meaning.

---

[30] http://data.worldbank.org/indicator/SP.DYN.LE00.IN

[31] Using data from UN Demographic Yearbook Reher defined onset of fertility decline as follows: It "has been set at the beginning of the first quinquennium after a peak, where fertility declines by at least 8% over two quinquennia and never increases again to levels approximating the original take-off point" (Reher, 2004, p.21)

[32] This measures contains negative values if the demographic transition lies in the future an spositive values if a country has already undergone the demographic transition.

[33] WDI 1960-2011 and Reher 1865-2000

3.1.2. Data on democracy

The data on democracy stem from the Polity IV project, which codes authority characteristics of polities all over the world. In defining "polity" the polity IV user's manual (Marshall, 2011, p.1) refers to Webster's New College Dictionary, which states that a polity is a "political or governmental organization; a society or institution with an organized government; state; body politic." Two different variables out of this dataset are employed in this paper. First of all, the eleven-point scale (0-10) of „institutionalized democracy" (democ), which is conceived as three different elements: Competitiveness and openness of executive recruitment, constraint of chief executive and competitiveness of political participation.

The second one is the combined polity score (polity2), which is computed by subtracting the institutionalized autocracy score from the institutionalized democracy score. Thus, its scale ranges from -10 (strongly autocratic) to +10 (strongly democratic)[34]. In this context, a value between +1 and +6 is considered as partial democracy and one between +7 and +10 as full democracy. But this measure also has its limitations because "autocratic and democratic authority are distinct patterns of authority, elements of which may co-exist in any particular regime context" (Marshall, 2011, p.17). The computation of this variable, however, implies that autocracy and democracy are alternatives that do not exist together. That means that the scores in the middle of the range can reflect completely different political situations and a "2" in one country can therefore not be easily compared to a "2" in another country[35].

3.1.3. Other data

Besides a couple of control variables, there remain four variables of interest: education, urbanization, women's empowerment and GDP per capita.

The World Development Indicators (WDI) provide multiple variables measuring education, from which data on school enrollment are most suitable for the purposes of this paper. The Gross enrollment ratio, which is taken for primary and secondary education, is the ratio "of total enrollment, regardless of age, to the population of the age group that officially corresponds to the level of education shown[36]". While these data are available since 1960 in 1-year intervals, Barro-Lee's schooling data (2011), which are cited in many major works on education, are given in 5-year intervals since 1800. On the one hand the advantage of the WDI school enrollment data is that they cover more countries more regularly than Barro-Lee's data; on the other hand they only go back to 1960 and are therefore not comparable with data from other sources before 1960.

---

34 A summary of the democracy variables is given in appendix C as well.

35 A polity score of "2" may result out of democracy score of 10 and autocracy score of 8 as well as out of a democracy score of 3 and a autocracy score of 1.

36 http://data.worldbank.org/indicator/SE.PRM.ENRR

They do also not reflect the educational level as precisely as Barro-Lee's estimation for average years of school attained because they only refer to primary or secondary education, whereas Barro-Lee's focus is on school attainment in general regardless of the schooling level. Limitations of Barro-Lee's dataset on the other hand are the smaller number of countries, missing observations and the 5-year intervals. Comparing them with other data that only exists since 1960 (as, for example, most demographic data used in this paper) the number of observations is likely to be narrowed down too much.

Urban population according to the WDI dataset "refers to people living in urban areas as defined by national statistical offices."[37] The variable is calculated as the ratio between people living in cities, estimated by the United Nations World Urbanization Prospects, and the total population. As an alternative measure Bank's urban population data[38] were employed, which unfortunately only contain few observations and therefore differ significantly from WDI data. Since the proportion of urban population on total population is a robust measure most tests were undertaken with these WDI data.

Finding a scale for women's empowerment is rather difficult because no such index exists for the past at least 50 years across different countries. Female labor force participation is taken as a proxy since it is a major component of the female emancipation process. The World Development Indicators, again, provide two indicators for this topic. On the one hand the labor participation rate, which is the economically active female population as percentage of the total above 15 female population, and on the other hand the ratio of female labor force and the total labor force. The former is used in most analyses because it best denotes the effect of working women compared to the whole female population.

Data on GDP per capita were available in almost every dataset[39], but in order to have as many matching observations as possible the focus here lies on the economic indicators drawn from the WDI database mainly[40].

---

[37] http://data.worldbank.org/indicator/SP.URB.TOTL.IN.ZS

[38] Description: "Population, Cities of 100,000 & Over Per Capita multiplied by 0.001"

[39] World Development Indicators (2011), Barro (2011), Banks (2007), Acemoglu (2007).

[40] Summary statistics of all additional variables can be found in appendix C as well.

3.2. Descriptive statistics

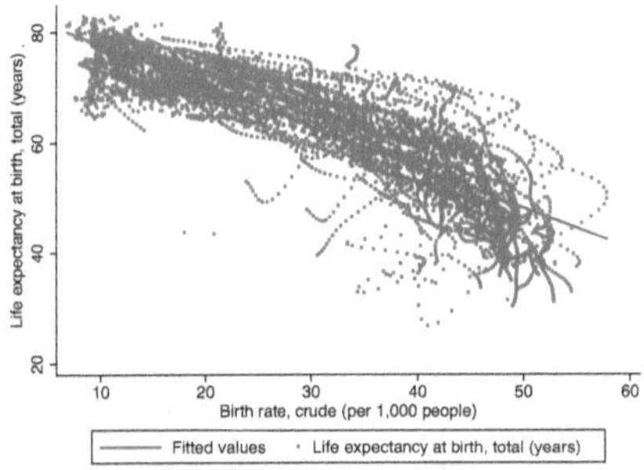

Figure 2 Life expectancies and birth rates

Figure 2 shows that high life expectancies are correlated with small crude birthrates[41]. Thus, the data in the dataset support the strong negative relationship between life expectancies and fertility rates, which is one of the main predictions theory makes about the demographic transition. Increasing life expectancies and declining birth rates as main characteristics of the demographic transition influence many economic and societal factors. Those consequences that potentially affect democracy in the end were presented in previous sections. There is also evidence in the data that there exist correlations between the demographic transition (here measured in years since the demographic transition, with negative values if the demographic transition lies in the future) and education, GDP per capita, female labor force participation and urban population, which are displayed in figure 3.

[41] The correlation coefficient is -0.875.

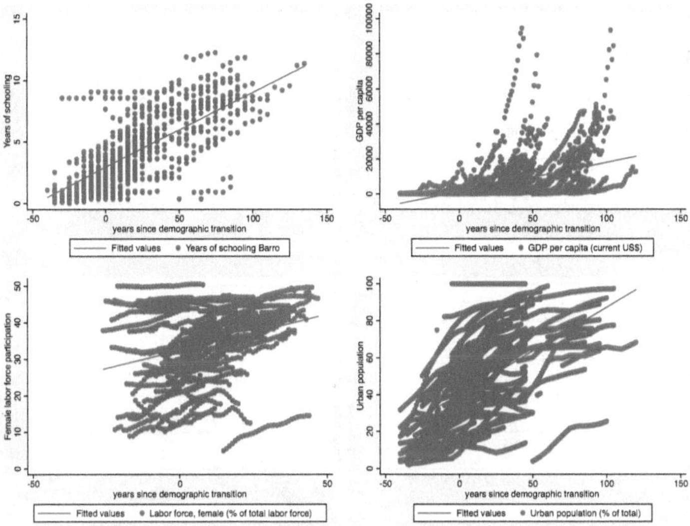

Figure 3 Consequences of the demographic transition

Correlations between these factors and democratization are shown in figure 4.

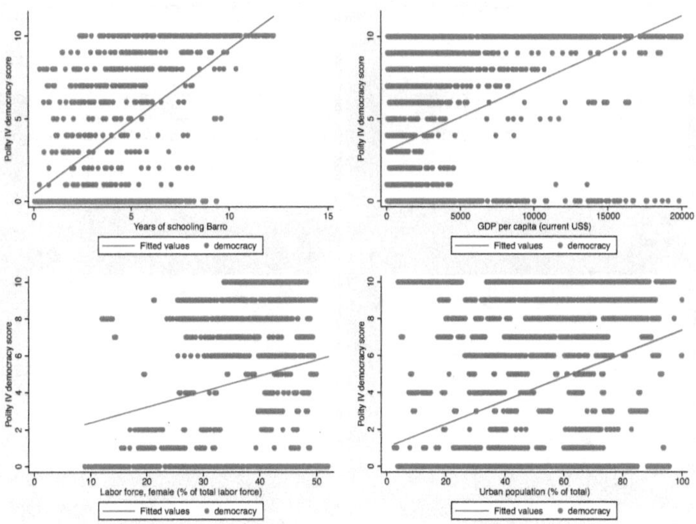

Figure 4 Determinants of democracy

All figures include – if available- comprehensive information of the datasets from 1800 until 2010, which gives them time independent validity and hence show a general pattern that can be applied for countries all over the world. Education, income, women's empowerment and urbanization are at the same time correlated with the demographic transition and democracy. Thus, a relationship between demography and democracy through these factors can be assumed. In order to characterize this relationship, however, following sections will provide a more profound econometrical framework.

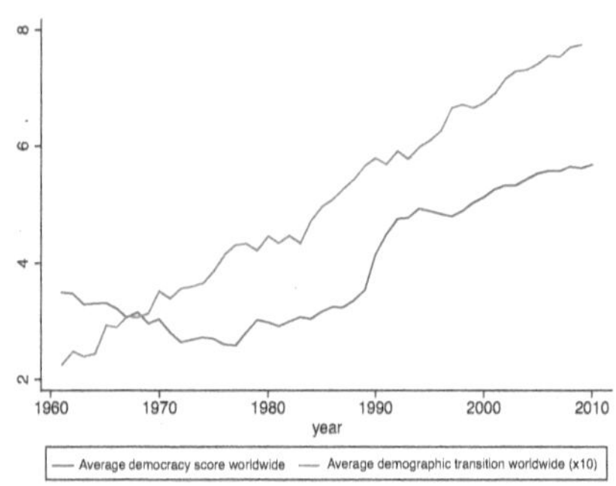

Figure 5 Development of democracy and demography

The direct relationship between the demographic transition and democracy is illustrated in figure 5. Observations since 1960 show that the accumulated number of demographic transitions and democracy scores follow the same trend over time. Figure 5 illustrates this trend by comparing the average Polity IV democracy index of all countries of the sample with the cross-country average of the binary variable "demotran" (multiplied by 10 in order to have the same scale as the democracy score) for each year. Moreover, the mean of the democracy variable for countries that have not experienced the demographic transition in the respective years is considerably smaller (2.57) than for countries that have passed the demographic transition in respective years (6.01)[42].

[42] See appendix C

4. Empirical analysis

The descriptive statistics show relationships between the demographic transition, democracy and the different channels as suggested in the theoretical part of this paper. However, to obtain evidence on the hypotheses constructed in section 2, econometric models have to be analyzed.

4.1. OLS model

4.1.1. Methodology

The goal of this section is to estimate the effect of the demographic transition on democracy and the role of different channels as stated in section 2 with empirical methods. Therefore, initially basic OLS estimates are computed using different dependent (democracy and polity2) and also different independent ("demotran" and "yearssincedt") variables. Since the demographic transition does not affect democracy immediately but with a time lag the binary regressor "demotran" is included with its 10- and 20-year lags[43] and so are in the further course other control variables. According to Dyson (2010) it takes almost one generation for social transitions to process and therefore, 10- and 20-year lags were chosen to account for this time delay. In addition, Reher (2011, p.22) detected that it takes the demographic transition on average a bit more than 20 years to pass trough. Due to the restricted time horizon of observations (often only 1960-2010 in 5-year intervals) including a higher number of lags than 20 was not possible.

Besides a sample with yearly observations another one, which contains 5- and 10-year intervals in order to have a bigger variance among the data, was examined. Also, cross-sectional analyses were conducted.

Based on section 2.1 the demographic transition is assumed to come mainly from outside the model and is also not explained by the model. Nevertheless, log(GDP per capita) is usually included as the most important control variable because it is very likely that omitted variable bias would arise otherwise. Even though the demographic transition is presupposed exogenously income still influences health to a certain degree and thereby the demographic transition while it also determines democracy. Gradually other controls such as the previous identified channels

[43] Regressions with all 20 lags of demotran (L(1/20)) have been run as well and yield similar results as regressions that include only the 10th and the 20th lag. Detailed information are reported in appendix D.1 or can be taken from the do-file.

that might be correlated with the demographic transition on the one hand and that are determinants of democracy on the other hand are included as well. Additionally, some models contain lags of democracy to account for autocorrelation.

Furthermore, heteroskedasticity robust standard errors are used because the homoskedasticity assumption[44] is likely to be violated and "violations of this assumption can invalidate statistical inferences" (Hayes&Cai, 2007, p.710). Even though the estimates would remain unbiased the „use of an HCSE [heteroskedasticity- consistent standard error] estimator, rather than assuming homoskedasticity when conducting inferential tests in OLS regression, can give the researcher greater comfort in the validity and power of those tests" (Hayes&Cai, 2007, p.716).

Accordingly, the equation of the OLS model is the following: $y_{it} = \beta_1 * x_{it} + \beta_2 * Z_{it} + \epsilon_{it}$, where y denotes the level of democracy in country i and year t, x the demographic transition, Z a vector for control variables and ε the error term.

4.1.2. Analysis

Dependent variable	democracy	democracy	democracy	Polity2democ (binary)	democracy	democracy
Estimation Model	OLS	OLS	OLS	Probit	OLS	OLS
Standard errors	HR	HR	HR	HR	HR	HR
Demotran (Demographic transition)	0.84 (0.25)***	.568 (0.272)**	.0585 (0.83)	-.14		
L10	2.83 (0.28) ***	.842 (0.35)**	.94 (1.2)	.522***		
L20	0.71 (0.33)***	2.285 (0.3)***	1.36 (0.8)**	.35**		
Years since demotran					0.06 (0.003)***	.0257 (0.014)**
Controls		Lgdppc, l10.lgdppc, l20.lgdppc	L(1/20)Lgdppc L(1/20).demotran	Gdppc (L10,L20), urbanpop (L10, L20), schoolenrollpri (L10,L20)	Lgdppc	Lgdppc, school, urbanpop, laboftotfem
n	2015	1871	1407	1060	2456	200
Adjusted R^2	0.22	0.28	0.26		0.38	0.44

Table 1 OLS model

*In parentheses, t-statistics based on heteroskedastic-consistent standard errors. ***,**,* denote 1%, 5% and 10% significance levels respectively. Whole sample is used.*

Detailed results of the OLS model are presented in appendix D.1. Following, the most important findings are highlighted.

[44] The variance of the conditional distribution of the error term ε_i given X_i is the same across X_i, so it does not depend on X_i (Stock&Watson, 2007, p.162).

The basic OLS model with polity2 or democracy as dependent variables yield statistically significant coefficients (on the 5% level) on the binary demographic transition variable and most of its lags. Adding control variables to these models increases the adjusted R^2 and the 10- and 20-year lags of the demographic transition stay significant while the current values of "demotran" become insignificant. Since it is unlikely that the demographic transition affects democracy immediately, the lags are more important than the current "demotran" value, and the coefficients on current "demotran" can be neglected. A probit- model with polity2 transformed into a binary variable[45] and a group of controls gives significant results for the lags on "demotran" as well. Thus, dichotomization does not change the results significantly. A binary variable can be useful to eliminate unknown contamination (Shentu& Xi, 200) and to obtain valid results if there are clusters on the boarders of the sample. However, "dichotomizing democracy lumps together countries with very different degrees of democracy and blurs distinctions between borderline cases" (Bollen& Jackman, 1989 p.612) and it causes a loss of useful information. Therefore, following analyses only include democracy as a continuous variable.

The focus of the analysis of the 5- and 10- year interval sample and the cross-sectional regression as presented in appendix D.1 also lies on the coefficients of the lags of the demographic transition. The coefficients on the 20-year lag on "demotran" in a cross-sectional regression for the year 2010 as well as in the 5- and 10-year interval model are significant. This means that when allowing for greater variance as in the interval-model or concentrating only on one year within the sample, it still holds true that the demographic transition has a positive influence on democracy around 20 years after its occurrence.

The coefficients on "demotran" in all these models lie in a range between 0.7 and 2.5, which means that the democracy level increases by up to 2.5 points[46] within the following 10 to 20 years after a country passed through the demographic transition. These results, however, only refer to countries that experienced their demographic transition after 1960 while the following analysis of the years-since-demographic-transition variable has validity for the longer time period covered in Reher's sample.

Using the continuous variable "years since demographic transition" yield statistically significant results regardless if the whole sample or 5- and 10-year intervals are examined. Cross-sectional models for 1960, 1980 and 2000 show that the effect of the demographic transition stays statistically significant in all cases.

---

45 Dichotomizing polity2: democracy=1 if polity2>6 (in accordance with Hegre et al.)

46 Out of 11, with "democracy" as dependent variable and out of 21, with "polity2" as dependent variable

Hence, the base OLS model predicts a statistically significant increase in democracy the more years since the demographic transition have passed.

One of the biggest challenges in estimating the effect of the demographic transition on democracy is potential omitted variable bias (OVB)[47]. GDP per capita, education, urbanization and female labor force participation do not capture all sources of bias since numerous other factors potentially influence a country's demographic as well as its political situation. In order to ensure exogeneity of the demographic transition these factors have to be examined more systematically. First of all, geographical factors are likely to influence the demographic transition because climate, the likelihood of natural catastrophes and a country's topography effect mortality rates and life expectancies. These same factors on the other hand also constitute political challenges and determine the most suitable ruling style as, for example, vast and remote areas are more difficult to control and rule than others. Secondly, political factors such as ideologies and previous political systems are correlated with the health level because they affect the governmental and private health expenditures. At the same time they also determine the current political system. Furthermore, the colonial past plays an important role for the health system as well as for present political institutions.

Thirdly, economic aspects besides GDP per capita, as for example inequalities, are correlated with health and thereby, with the demographic transition and also democracy. The coverage with medicine, for instance, depends on income equality and income distribution on the one hand and on the other hand income inequality is a source of social conflict, which makes democracy less tenable (Lipest, 1959).

Furthermore, other in literature discussed causes of democracy like religion, ethnologic fragmentation or population density can also be interpreted in the light of demography. Certain religions or ethnologic groups, for example, have special rites that influence health, mortality and fertility rates. Hence, in order to ensure the highest exogeneity possible the model has to control for these factors.

[47] "Omitted variable bias is the bias in the OLS estimator that arises when the regressor, X, is correlated with an omitted variable. For omitted variable bias to occur, two conditions must be true:

1. X is correlated with the omitted variable
2. The omitted variable is a determinant of the dependent variable, Y. "

(Stock&Watson, 2007, p.189)

4.2. Country fixed effects

4.2.1. Methodology

All these aforementioned aspects from geographical over political to economic factors, are country specific and can therefore be controlled for with country fixed effects, which eliminate all sources of bias that arise from variables that are country-specific[48]. "The key insight is that if the unobserved variable does not change over time, then any changes in the dependent variable must be due to influences other than these fixed characteristics." (Stock & Watson, 2003, p.289-290). Thus, a more credible model to estimate the effect of the demographic transition on democracy is a panel model using country fixed effects since OLS estimates are probably biased due to OVB. That is, a model of the following form: $y_{it} = \beta_1 * x_{it} + \beta_2 * Z_{it} + \mu_t + \epsilon_{it}$, which only differs from the basic OLS-model because of the full set of country dummies μ_t.

In panel data with fixed effects the assumption of independent and identically distributed (iid) observations is loosened and it is instead assumed that clusters are iid (Stock&Watson, 2007, p.364). That is because observations are independent from observations of any other unit, however not independent within a unit. This implies that covariances within a cluster may not be zero, which is called autocorrelation[49]. Therefore, in all fixed effect models heteroskedasticity and autocorrelation robust standard errors (HAC) are used.

4.2.2. Analysis

Expanding the model by including country fixed effects also results in statistically significant coefficients on the lags of "demotran" whether poilty2 or democracy is used as dependent variable. Adding log(gdp per capita) and its lags to the model the coefficients on "demotran" become insignificant. This could be a sign that the over time varying economic situation, which is not captured by the country fixed effects biased the former results because it is correlated to the demographic transition and to democracy. Therefore, interactions between income and the demographic transition are examined in section 4.3.2. Besides the economic situation it is also likely that the educational level is an omitted variable in this equation and therefore, the next regression estimates coefficients on "demotran" with years of schooling and its lags included as controls. This yields a significant coefficient on the 20-year lag of the demographic transition. Adding more controls is not possible because then there are not sufficient observations left for

---

48 varying across country but not across time

49 "If u_{it} is correlated with u_{is} for different values of t and s- that is, if u_{it} is correlated over time for a given entity-then u_{it} is said to be autocorrelated (correlated with itself at different dates)" (Stock&Watson, 2007, p.366)

valid estimations. GDP per capita, schooling and country-specific factors are the most important determinants of democracy that are correlated with the demographic transition. Thus, they ensure a high degree of exogeneity and therefore, this model is considered as highly convincing.

Dependent variable	democracy	democracy	democracy	democracy	democracy
Estimation Model	Country FE	Country FE	Country FE	Country FE	Country FE
Standard errors	HAC	HAC	HAC	HAC	HAC
Demotran (Demographic transition)	0.22 (0.39)	0.03 (0.44)	.316 (.64)		
L10	0.78 (0.56)*	0.37 (0.65)	.898 (1.05)		
L20	1.32 (0.76)**	0.82 (0.78)	3.6 (1.6)**		
Years since demotran				0.1 (0.02)***	.102 (0.042)**
Controls		Lgdppc, l10.lgdppc, l20.lgdppc	Lgdppc, l10.lgdppc, l20.lgdppc school, l10.school, l20.school	lgdppc	Lgdppc, school
n	2015 (75 countries)	1871 (71 countries)	182 (47 countries)	2456 (60 countries)	330 (42 countries)
R^2	.04	.1	0.23	0.2	0.15

Table 2 Country fixed effects

*(In parentheses, t-statistics based on heteroskedastic-consistent standard errors. ***,**,* denote 1%, 5% and 10% significance levels respectively. Whole sample is used.)*

Splitting the effect of the demographic transition up into its components- life expectancies and crude birth rates- provides a deeper insight into the mechanism how the effect of the demographic transition works. The results (in appendix D.2) show that the coefficient on demographic transition becomes insignificant, the coefficients on the lags of the components, however, are significant with the expected sign (life expectancy positive and crude birth rates negative). The result remains approximately the same even when log(gdp per capita) and its lags are added as control variables. That the coefficients on the demographic transition itself become insignificant when adding its components is reasonable since the effect on democracy works through higher life expectancies and lower birth rates. The comparatively high coefficients on life expectancy emphasize the importance of longer life perspectives and life experience for democratizations.

Having analyzed the effect of mortality and birth rates separately the focus now turns back to the effect of the demographic transition as a whole. While the coefficient on the binary independent variable "demotran" is positive but insignificant when controlling for log(GDP per capita), employing years since demographic transition as independent variable results in a statistically significant coefficient. Even when years of schooling as second control is added the coefficient stays significant. These regressions are more convincing than regressions with demographic transition as binary variable because the continuous independent variable leaves more room for variation as it distinguishes between each year that passed since the demographic transition. Moreover it covers a longer time span. Thus the number of observations is 2456 (respectively 330 including Barro's schooling data), while the other one covers only 1871 and 187 observations respectively. Hence, these models are more representative and most reliable.[50]

In conclusion, this first set of estimations shows that the demographic transition has a statistically significant influence on democracy amounting to around 2 points within 20 years on average on the democracy scale when considering the binary variable "demographic transition" and its lags and approximately 0.1 points when accounting for years passed since the demographic transition. When controlling for country-specific factors, income and education the demographic transition can be classified as nearly exogenous, which ensures that the model computes exactly the effect we are interested in, namely the effect of the demographic transition on democracy. Since coefficients in the majority of the respective models on both variables are significantly positive, the positive relationship between the demographic transition or the time that has passed since the demographic transition and democracy has been verified. Thus, hypothesis one[51], which was constructed in section 2, is proven empirically.

4.3. Robustness check

This section examines how the core regression coefficient estimates, identified in section 4.2, behave when the econometrical framework is modified. As important modifications the inclusion of time fixed effects, interactions with income and the timing of the demographic transition are considered. Firstly, using time fixed effects is always an option when analyzing panel data, because they control for factors that are constant across countries but vary over time and thereby reduce the threat of OVB. Thus, it can be useful to find out how the estimates change when time

50 For a detailed overview over all results see appendix D.2

51 (1.) The demographic transition has a positive influence on the rise of democracy

FE are added. Secondly, previous sections pointed out that income is an important factor that possibly interacts with the demographic transition and hence, this interaction is included into the model. Finally, the time of the demographic transition plays a major role regarding the effect of the demographic transition on democracy because in some countries the onset of the demographic transition occurred 100 years earlier than in others. Thus, the societal context was a completely different one and estimates might therefore depend on the timing.

4.3.1. Year fixed effects

As a robustness check, time fixed effects are included in the model since one could think of factors varying over time but not across countries that might cause OVB. Such factors could be the world economic situation, changing attitudes towards more liberal thinking in terms of health and politics in modern times and worldwide innovations. The time fixed effects models are only robustness checks because it seems rather unlikely that these factors are constant across all countries. Moreover, integrating country and time fixed effects eliminates much information and reduces therefore the validity of the model.
The estimation equation of this model includes the new component time fixed effects (ζ_i) and hence has the form: $y_{it} = \beta_1 * x_{it} + \beta_2 * Z_{it} + \mu_t + \zeta_i + \epsilon_{it}$

Using the binary independent variable "demotran" the country and year fixed effects model does not yield any reasonable results. Either coefficients are insignificant or the coefficient on the demographic transition variable becomes negatively significant. The coefficients on the lags, however, stay mostly positive, which indicates that the long-term effects of the demographic transition on democracy are positive, as expected, and the current state of the demographic transition absorbs omitted variables that are negatively correlated with democracy. One reason for the insignificance of these results could be that that the coefficients on demographic transition in former regressions are identified from overtime variations. Those are factors that are related to the joint evolution of economic, demographic and political development, which are the same in every country but vary over time. Also, most of the variation is taken out of the model through country and time fixed effects and thus, predictions become vague. Since "demotran" is a binary variable its validity is already restricted because it does not allow for any nuances regarding the process of the demographic transition. Once all time- and country-specific factors are taken out of this model there is not much explanation power left, which could account for variances in democracy. Hence, the model using a binary regressor is sensitive towards time fixed effects.

Shifting the focus towards the continuous independent variable model with country and year fixed effects, however, reinforces the results from previous estimations. The coefficients on years since demographic transition are statistically significant whether only log(GDP per capita) or both log(GDP per capita) and years of schooling are included in the regression. Only the magnitude of the coefficients lowers a bit from 0.1 in the country fixed effect model to 0.06 and 0.08 in country-and year fixed effect model. This means in terms of democracy scores that within 10 years after the demographic transition democracy level rises by 0.6 or 0.8 points[52].

The different results of the binary and continuous independent variable could be due to the different samples underlying these two models.

The results estimated in the country fixed effect model are robust at least for the continuous independent variable not only when controlling for country-specific factors, income and education but also for time-specific factors. Most of the following analyses therefore use "years since demographic transition" as regressor and thereby refer to all countries contained in Reher's sample.

Dependent variable	democracy	democracy	democracy	democracy	democracy
Time/Country FE?	Country FE, year FE	Country FE, year FE	Country FE, Time FE	Country FE, Time FE	Country FE, Time FE
Standard errors	HAC	HAC	HAC	HAC	HAC
Demotran (Demographic transition)	-1.2 (0.49)*	-1.1 (0.5)*			
L10	-0.07 (0.6)	0.02 (0.7)			
L20	0.06 (0.7)	0.13 (0.8)			
Years since demotran			0.02 (0.006)***	0.06 (0.02)**	.084 (.039)**
Controls		Lgdppc (L10, L20)		lgdppc	Lgdppc, school
n	2015 (75 countries)	1424 (63 countries)	12895 (135 countries)	2456 (60 countries)	330 (42 countries)
R^2	0.2	0.2	0.3	0.23	0.17

Table 3 Country and year fixed effects

*(In parentheses, t-statistics based on heteroskedastic-consistent standard errors. ***,**,* denote 1%, 5% and 10% significance levels respectively. Whole sample is used.)*

52 All results of combined country and year-fixed effects regressions are presented in appendix D.3.

4.3.2. Interactions with income

As stated before, a countries' economic situation plays an important role in measuring the effect of demography on democracy and therefore, the next part of the analysis focuses on interactions between the demographic transition and GDP per capita. In addition, the sample is divided in „rich" countries, which are defined as countries that have a higher GDP per capita than the sample's mean per capita income (6000$) and „poor" ones, whose GDP per capita is below the mean. It is also possible that a country is initially considered as poor but passes the threshold at one point and is therefore, classified as rich in subsequent observations. For this purpose the country fixed effect model with log(GDP per capita) as control is applied because it has proven to be the most reliable one. Thereof, arises the following equation, with g_{it} as GDP per capita in country i at time t: $y_{it} = \beta_1 * x_{it} + \beta_2 * g_{it} + \beta_3 * x_{it} * g_{it} + \beta_4 * Z_{it} + \mu_t + \epsilon_{it}$

The estimation yields the result that interactions between income per capita and the binary variable "demotran" as well as with the continuous variable years since demographic transition are negatively significant. This means that the effect of the demographic transition on democracy is stronger the smaller a country's income. This result is supported when dividing the sample in a below and an above mean income group. Using the country fixed effects model developed in section 4.2[53] the coefficient in the above mean income group is considerably smaller (0.009) and not even significant compared to the coefficient in the below mean income group (0.11), which is significant on a 5% level.

It is likely that in poorer countries the effects of the demographic transition are stronger than in rich countries because a high national income already ensures a certain development level of factors that influence democracy[54]. Namely, many of the outcomes of the demographic transition that eventually lead to democracy such as education, urbanization and women's empowerment are at the same time determined by income. Assuming that these factors that determine democracy have diminishing marginal products, the room for improvements through the demographic transition is much smaller in rich than in poor countries. This means that the effect of the consequences of a demographic transition on democracy is weaker in rich than in poor countries. If, for example, a country is rich it is likely that it has a higher level of education than a poor country. A demographic transition, then, can improve the educational level in the poor

53 $y_{it} = \beta_1 * x_{it} + \beta_2 * Z_{it} + \mu_t + \epsilon_{it}$

54 Many factors that determine democracy are also influenced by income such as education, income equality, urbanization, trade and historical factors (Sunde, 2006, p.14-18). The positive influence income has on democracy is referred to as the so called "Aristotele-Lipset-Hypothesis (Sunde, 2006, p.14)

country by much more than in the rich country. Hence, the effect of income on democracy dominates in rich countries while in poor countries the outcomes of the demographic transition play a major role.

	Full sample	Full sample	Full sample	Rich countries (gdppc>6000)	Poor countries (gdppc<6000)
Dependent Variable	democracy Country FE	democracy Country FE	democracy Country FE	democracy Country FE	democracy Country FE
Standard Errors	HAC	HAC	HAC	HAC	HAC
Yearssincedt	. 087 (0.016)***		.1 (0.02)***	.0092 (.007)	.112 (.021)***
Yearssincedt*gdppc	-.0000521 (.0000259)**				
demotran		1.33(0.48)***			
Demotran*gdppc		-.0000893 (.0000412)**			
gdppc		.000119 (.0000465) **			
Controls	lgdppc		lgdppc	lgdppc	lgdppc
n	2401 (60 countries)	2767 (73 countries)	2456 (60 countries)	444 (20 countries)	2012 (60 countries)
R^2	0.2	0.04	0.2	0.01	0.22

Table 4 Interactions with income

*(In parentheses, t-statistics based on heteroskedastic-consistent standard errors. ***,**,* denote 1%, 5% and 10% significance levels respectively.)*

4.3.3. Time of demographic transition

Another reason for the differences estimated in 4.3.2 is that most of the developed and rich countries are at the same time so-called forerunners and thus, not only income but also the timing of the demographic transition might influence the effect of the demographic transition on democracy.

In order to verify this argument the sample is divided again, this time according to the Reher-groups. While the influence of the demographic transition on democracy in the forerunner group is the smallest (0.01) and not significant, the coefficient on the demographic transition becomes significant on a 5% level and bigger (0.086) in the combined followers and trailers group and in the latecommer group the influence of years since the demographic transition on democracy is the biggest (0.12) and most significant one (1% level). Hence, these results confirm that hypothesis I holds true for countries whose demographic transition and subsequent democratizations took place in the second half of the 20th century or later, however, not for the "forerunners" who experienced the first wave democratization process[55].

There are two possible reasons for these different effects at different times: Either the outcomes of the demographic transition or the determinants of democracy in the late 19th and early 20th century differ compared to those in the second half of the 20th century. According to Reher (2011, p. 13) the decline of death and birth rates in recent transitions is much faster than the decline in historic transitions. Furthermore, the gap between mortality and fertility decline is much larger in recent times. This is due to the fact that the latest demographic transitions are characterized by much more progressed technologies and techniques, which are more efficient than historic instruments. Thus, the gap becomes larger and the changes take place faster. This also influences the outcomes of the demographic transition since they are produced faster and the magnitude of these effects is higher. Hence, faster and more efficient demographic transitions in recent times explain the stronger effect of the demographic transition on societal outcomes and thereby, on democracy in the follower, trailer and latecomer groups in contrast to the forerunner group.

It is, however, also likely that the relevance of the determinants of democracy differs over time[56]. Other factors contributed to the first wave democratizations than to later waves since the political and societal situation was completely different at that time and globalization has not been as progressed as in the second half of the 20th century. New communication technologies, broader information sources and global interconnectedness that on the one hand facilitate reform movements but on the other hand can also be used to suppress people, determined politics in the past 50 years. Therefore, factors such as education and women's empowerment become even more important for democratization movements in a globalized world as people have to be able to use these new opportunities. The higher a country's educational level is the more people can participate in the political system and the more likely is a democracy to occur. In former times, however, people had less information sources, hierarchical systems ruled and they could not

[55] This result is also confirmed by the significant results of the basic OLS and country fixed effect models using the binary regressor "demotran" and its lags, which only refer to countries that experienced their demographic transition after 1960.

[56] Most major works on democracy only examine democratization processes of a certain time period, as for example Huntington (1991) with his analysis of the third wave democratization. These different focuses show that democratization processes at different times can hardly be compared and thus, the determinants must also work in different ways.

communicate easily among each other; thus, even for educated people there was not much room for political participation, which means that it could not influence democracy as much as during the second and third waves of democratization. Hence, different societal situations affect the determinants of democracy at different times.

Moreover, the influence of demography on democracy is more reliable for recent than for historic transition processes because the demographic transition in the 19th and early 20th century was largely endogenous driven[57]. Thus, simultaneous causality between the demographic transition and democracy are a threat to the results at that time. As analyzed before, in modern times, causality from democracy to the demographic transition does not play a major role anymore since the international community ensures a basic health level in every country.

In addition, the forerunners experienced their demographic transition already at the beginning of the 20th century or even earlier and most observations in the dataset for these countries lie far behind their demographic transition. Therefore, most values for the independent variable "years since demographic transition" are very high and not correlated with democracy scores anymore. This results in a weak overall relationship between years since demographic transition and democracy for these countries. To adjust for this bias, only observations until, for example, 50 years[58] after the demographic transition should be included in the sample.

It is important to note, that these findings only refer to models using years since demographic transition as independent variable because these data start already in 1890 while data employed for the binary independent variable "demotran" only start in 1960 and therefore, only focus on recent transitions.

With the methods employed in this paper it is impossible to distinguish if a country's income or the date of its demographic transition are the trigger for different effects of the demographic transition on democracy. That is, because most rich countries belong to the forerunner-group while poorer countries experienced their demographic transition in more recent times.
It is, however, likely that it is a combination of these two factors. On the one hand the different environment in the early 20th century certainly has an influence on the effect of the demographic

[57] The influence of democracy (which leads to simultaneous causality problems) and income, for example, on the demographic transition played a major role at these times.
[58] Because 50 years after the demographic transition the relevant factors (education, income, urbanization, women empowerment) should have adjusted and exercised their influence on democracy

transition on democracy and on the other hand a country's income level also determines which effect the demographic transition can have on democracy.

Group	Full sample	Forerunner (before 1935)	Followers & Trailers (1950-1979)	Latecommers (after 1980)
Dependent variable	democracy	democracy	democracy	democracy
	Country FE	Country FE	Country FE	Country FE
Standard Errors	HAC	HAC	HAC	HAC
Yearssincedt	.1 (0.02)***	.0112 (0.053)	.086 (0.0339)**	.1239 (.031)***
Controls	lgdppc	lgdppc	lgdppc	lgdppc
n	2456 (60 countries)	533 (12 countries)	1033 (24 countries)	708 (20 countries)
Adjusted R^2	0.2	0.09	0.22	0.25

Table 5 Time of demographic transition

*(In parentheses, t-statistics based on heteroskedastic-consistent standard errors. ***,**,* denote 1%, 5% and 10% significance levels respectively.)*

4.4. How the demographic transition affects democracy

The second part of the empirical analysis turns towards testing hypothesis number two: Through which channels affects the demographic transition democracy? Before executing a channel analysis on education, women's empowerment, income and urbanization the effects of the individual parts of the demographic transition- life expectancy and birth rates- are tested.

4.4.1. Life expectancy and birth rates

After testing the effect of the demographic transition on democracy in general the effect of the components of the demographic transition, namely life expectancies and crude birth rates, are again tested separately. Life expectancies and crude birthrates are tested on the basis of different models (OLS and fixed effect models) with different dependent variables. However, only 10-year lags are included in this model because these regressors develop their full effects faster than the more restrictive defined variable of the demographic transition.

Examining the effect of life expectancies and crude birthrates separately, yield positive significant coefficients on the lag of log(life expectancy) in all models and negative, sometimes significant, coefficients on the lag of log(crude birth rates). The most reliable models out of the whole set are regressions controlling for both income and education and including country or even year fixed effects. While log(life expectancy) is significant even on a 1% level, crude birth rates are negative but not significant and rather small (around -0.1). This result implies that the main driver of the influence of the demographic transition on democracy is life expectancy. The coefficients on log(life expectancy) in these two models lie between 6 and 8, which means that a 10% increase in life expectancies leads to an increase of approximately 0.7 points on the democracy scale after ten years[59]. This supports the thesis that higher life expectancies and thereby, more life perspectives on the one hand and more life experiences on the other hand, promote democracy. Higher life expectancies as one outcome of the demographic transition also influence education and GDP per capita. It remains to be seen in the channel analysis if these two are also the most important channels through which the demographic transition affects democracy.

4.4.2. Channel analysis

The channel analysis is executed analogously to Tavares and Wacziarg (2001). First of all, a correlation matrix correlates democracy with all channel variables and the demographic transition and also the channel variables among themselves. It contains information on the relationships between democracy, years since demographic transition and the possible channels. All channels are, as expected, positively correlated with the demographic transition and democracy. Crude birth rates are in line with expectations negatively correlated because the lower the value of this indicator is, the higher are the values of the other variables. The highest correlations exist among the demographic variables. The correlation coefficient between life expectancies and crude birth rates amounts to -0.88, between years since the demographic transition and life expectancy to 0.73 and between years since demographic transition and crude birth rates to -0.82, which is reasonable since life expectancies and crude birth rates and their negative relationship are the underlying idea of the whole demographic transition theory. Also high correlations were obtained between school and crude birth rates (-0.8), life expectancies (0.76) and years since demographic transition (0.84). These results indicate a strong relationship between education and the demographic variables.

For the purpose of examining these relationships more closely, different regressions are executed. At first, country fixed effects models with different controls are employed in order to show the consequences of the demographic transition. The different suggested channels are used as dependent variables and the respective coefficients on the demographic transition are singled out. The equation system for this channel analysis looks as follows:

---

[59] An overview over the results is displayed in appendix D.6.

Consequences of the demographic transition (x_{it})[60]:

$$education_{it} = \gamma_1 * x_{it} + \gamma_2 * Z_{it} + \mu_t + \epsilon_{it}$$

$$urbanpop_{it} = \delta_1 * x_{it} + \delta_2 * Z_{it} + \mu_t + \epsilon_{it}$$

$$femaleparticipation_{it} = \eta_1 * x_{it} + \eta_2 * Z_{it} + \mu_t + \epsilon_{it}$$

$$gdppc_{it} = \theta_1 * x_{it} + \theta_2 * Z_{it} + \mu_t + \epsilon_{it}$$

As in the base model, this framework also has to deal with simultaneous causality problems. It is possible that the demographic transition itself is influenced by the factors constituting the dependent variable in this model. But –as stated in section 2- in this paper the dominant direction of causation is assumed to go from the demographic transition to education, urban population, women's empowerment and GDP, which cause democratization. On this basis, this part of the paper analyzes the significance of these relationships.

This yields the result that the demographic transition has a significant influence on all channels, even if country fixed effects and other controls are included. The effect of the demographic transition on school is 0.06, which means that 10 years further ago from the demographic transition rises the level of schooling by 0.6 years. 10 years further away from the demographic transition also leads to an increase of the urban population by 5 percentage points and the ratio between economically active women and total female population rises by 2 percentage points, which is a rather small change compared to the mean of this variable of 47%. The mean of GDP per capita amounts to approximately 6000$, thus, a coefficient of 202 on years since demographic transition indicates a strong positive effect of the demographic transition on GDP per capita.

Subsequently, a basic OLS model with democracy as dependent variable is executed and thereby, determinants of democracy are detected.

Determinants of democracy (y_{it}):

$$y_{it} = \kappa_1 * education_{it} + \kappa_2 * urbanpop_{it} + \kappa_3 * femaleparticpation_{it} + \kappa_4 * gdppc_{it} + \kappa_5 * Z_{it} + \epsilon_{it}$$

It yields that all channel variables except female labor force participation have a statistically significant influence on democracy. This, on the one hand, rejects the hypothesis that women's empowerment is an important channel that affects democracy but proves on the other hand that

[60] as regressor the continuous variable "years since demographic transition" is used.

education, urbanization and income have a statistically significant influence on democracy. Hence, the role of women in democratization processes is not as important as expected. This result, however, could be due to the fact that female labor force participation does not exactly represent a society's degree of women's empowerment. The variable is not even a measure for male/female equality because it does not take any male ratio into account as comparative measurements.

Channel	Effect of demographic transition on channel	Effect of channel on democracy	Effect of demographic transition on democracy
Education (school)	.0663(0.00695)***	.629 (0.1)***	0.0417
Urbanization (urbanpop)	.521 (0.0423)***	.0217 (0.0134)*	0.0113
Female laborforce participation (laboftotfem)	.2324 (0.0376)***	.01124 (0.01473)	-
GDP (gdppc)	201.8 (43.4)***	.0000915 (0.000032)**	0.0185
Total effect			0.0714

Table 6 Summary of channel analysis

*(In parentheses, t-statistics based on heteroskedastic-consistent standard errors. ***,**,* denote 1%, 5% and 10% significance levels respectively.)*

In order to quantify the effect of the demographic transition on democracy through each channel the coefficients on demographic transition are multiplied with the coefficients on the respective channels in the democracy model. This yields the result that the effects through education (0.04) and gdppc (0.02) are the strongest. This goes along with the results from section 4.4.1 (that demonstrate the importance of life expectancies for democratizations) because income and education are main outcomes of higher life expectancies.

The total effect of the demographic transition amounts to 0.07, which means that a 10-year time lag since the demographic transition increases the democracy score by 0.7 out of 10 points. This estimated total effect is very close to the estimate (0.1) from the former regression in section 4.2.2, where the direct effect of the demographic transition on democracy was estimated on the basis of a country fixed effect model controlling for log(GDP per capita). Since the indirect method introduced in this chapter only considers the effect through the channels, the proximity of the coefficients indicates that the suggested channels are the main drivers for the effect from the demographic transition to democracy.

Hence, hypothesis two[61] can be confirmed for income, education and urbanization as channels, is, however, not confirmed with respect to women's empowerment.

So all in all, a positive effect of the demographic transition on democracy could be proven, however only for low-income countries that experienced their demographic transition and following democratization process in the second half of the 20th century or later. The main driver of this effect are higher life expectancies, which promote broader perspectives regarding the value and opportunities of life for the people. This is reflected in higher participation rates and changing attitudes towards politics since politics determines the whole societal system. Moreover, higher life expectancies lead to a bigger and more productive labor force, which is a key source of economic growth. Higher incomes in turn affect democracy. Also the educational level rises as life expectancies increase, which is another important determinant of democracy. Thus, besides urbanization to a minor degree, education and income are the main channels through which the demographic transition affects democracy.

[61] (2.) The effect of the demographic transition on democracy works primarily through the channels of education, women's empowerment, urbanization and economic growth

5. Limitations

But there are still some limitations of the framework introduced in section 4.
The biggest problem arises from simultaneous causality between the demographic transition, the suggested channels and democracy. As stated in section 2.1 in modern, globalized times national health levels do not depend on the political system so much anymore, it can, however, not be ruled out that there exists any connection. A solution to this problem would be a suitable instrument for the demographic transition that is completely exogenous, which has not been found so far[62]. As long as such an instrument is not found one has to settle with the suggested estimation framework. Having suitable instruments also would have been useful for a 3SLS[63] channel analysis to account for endogeneity of income, education, urbanization and women's empowerment.
Since the estimated relationship between the demographic transition and democracy is more significant for the recent past than for historical times the problem is, however, alleviated because in modern times the health level and thereby, the demographic transition become more and more independent from the political system.

Moreover, the econometrical analysis in this paper is confined to linear models, but it is also plausible that the influence of the demographic transition on democracy follows a non-linear path. Not each year after the demographic transition has the same influence on democracy as the previous year. Immediately after the transition there is probably hardly any effect because it takes a society several years to adjust to the new situation and thus, democracy cannot be determined instantly. At one point, on the other hand, the effect disappears completely since the whole system has eventually adjusted. Between these two extremes the effect reaches its maximum at one point, which could be computed if a non-linear model was used. This approach remains for future research.

Even though fixed effects and suitable controls ensure the exogeneity of the demographic transition in the best possible way there is still the possibility that there exist factors that are correlated with the demographic transition as well as with democracy that vary across countries

62 Acemoglu et al. (2007) employed predicted mortality as an instrument for changes in life expectancies, which is not considered as a suitable for the demographic transition as it is defined in this paper because it does not fulfill both, the criterion of the instrument's relevance and its exogeneity. Furthermore, it is hardly applicable to today's situation since the epidemiological transition lies more than 70 years back.
63 Zellner&Theil (1962)

and over time, which could cause OVB. Since each model controls for per capita income[64] and country-specific factors the main sources of potential OVB are eliminated. Most results are even robust when controlling for the educational level and time-specific factors.

Furthermore, using panel data always goes along with challenges regarding data availability since not all countries have data of all indicators over time equally. Often richer countries have more information, especially about the past, which could cause sample selection bias. Moreover, merging different datasets, particularly WDI, Barro-Lee and Polity IV, leads to a loss of information on countries and years that do not appear in all three datasets. Barro-Lee's data, for example, are only available in 5-year intervals, while WDI provides only data since 1960. Thus, models that include schooling data from Barro-Lee as well as other information from WDI can only operate with observations from 1960 in 5-year intervals. It was, however, still necessary to merge these data because there does not exist one dataset with all relevant information and therefore these losses have to be accepted.

These limitations imply a partially restricted validity of the results. Most importantly, the empirical analysis does not allow a final comment about the direction of causality. Based on the theoretical part, however, the causation from the demographic transition to democracy is considered as the dominant one. Under this assumption the influence of the demographic transition on democracy in poor countries that experienced their demographic transition in the second half of the 20th century was identified as statistically significant. Even though the models contain above-mentioned limitations, they are nevertheless considered as accurate because they capture most sources of bias and the remaining sources are not big enough to invalidate the whole model.

[64] It is likely that income is correlated with the demographic transition because it has an influence on the health level (compare section 2.1 for a relativization of this assumption at least in modern times) and there exists empirical evidence that it is has an influence on democracy (Barro, 1999)

6. Conclusion

In order to identify the effect of the demographic transition on democracy the country fixed effect model controlling for income and education is considered the most reliable one because it ensures an unbiased and consistent estimator in the best possible way, given the data and methods used in this paper[65]. Furthermore the continuous variable "years since demographic transition" is preferred to a binary variable representing the occurrence of the demographic transition, as it is allows for greater variance, is more robust and represents more than 150 countries over a time span covering more than 150 years.

The demographic transition has a statistically significant influence on democracy in countries that experienced their demographic transition and subsequent democratization in the second half of the 20th century or later. This goes along with the finding that the effect is stronger in low- than in high-income countries since the demographic transition and democratization of most developed and rich countries already took place in the late 19th or early 20th century.
One possible explanation is that the effect of income on democracy in rich countries is stronger than in poor countries since income influences similar factors as the demographic transition that eventually determine democracy. Thus, there is not so much space for improvements through the demographic transition in rich countries. Therefore, in rich countries the direct effects of income on democracy probably outweigh the effects of a demographic transition. In addition, the political, economic and societal situation was completely different in the 19th and early 20th century compared to the second half of the 20th century. Thus, the effects of the demographic transition on society as well as the determinants of democracy differ over time.
Furthermore, the values for the variable "years since demographic transition" become extremely high for countries that experienced their demographic transition more than hundred years ago and at one point there does not exist a relationship between this variable and democracy scores anymore, which could be illustrated by non-linear models. Since, however, only linear models were used it cannot be accounted for this relationship and the results may be biased.

As another result of the analysis life expectancy was identified as the main driver of the effect of the demographic transition on democracy while crude birth rates only play a minor role. Higher

65 It particularly prevents OVB because country-specific factors, income and education are at the same time correlated with the demographic transition and might determine democracy (see section 4.4).

life expectancies in post-transitional times go along with more life perspectives and therefore, more awareness for the political system. Hence, attitudes towards opportunities of life and politics change during a demographic transition. Higher life expectancies also lead to higher investments in education and a more productive labor force, which eventually promotes economic growth and higher per capita incomes. The channel analysis supports this result as the estimated effect of the demographic transition on education and GDP per capita but also on urbanization are statistically significant positive. The effects of education and GDP per capita on democratization are, however, stronger than the effect of urbanization. Thus, the demographic transition affects democracy mainly through higher education and rising incomes. While women's empowerment has been identified as an outcome of the demographic transition it has no statistically significant influence on democracy. Hence, the hypothesis that women's empowerment can be employed as a channel through which the demographic transition affects democracy is not proven.

Besides the model specification the main limitation of the analysis is simultaneous causality. While all models control for country-specific factors and income, the exogeneity assumption might be violated because democracy also promotes the demographic transition to a certain degree. In modern times, however, it is probably only a minor determinant and as no suitable instrument for the demographic transition has been found the influence of the demographic transition on democracy as the dominant direction of causation is examined. Using different functional forms and instrumental variables leaves room for further research.

All in all, the demographic transition has been identified as a determinant of democracy in poor countries in modern times. But there are other factors that influence democracy as well, which have not been analyzed in this paper that should not be neglected when discussing about democracy. Furthermore, the results only state that the demographic transition and its consequences are favorable for democracy. No comment can be made about how they work exactly in different political systems at different stages of democratization processes.

Consequently, many African and Asian countries that have recently passed through or are about to pass through the demographic transition have now the opportunity to benefit from its positive effects on education and income, which may eventually lead to democracy. A guarantee for democratization processes in all post-transitional societies, does however, not exist.

The analyses presented in this paper extend Dyson's (2010) and Reher's (2011) theory about political implications of the demographic transition by using econometrical models in order to examine the positive effect of the demographic transition on democracy. It confirms that under certain circumstances "demographic change can and should be seen as an essential factor of change that has profound implications for society" (Reher, 2011), which are in this context favorable prerequisites for democratization movements. Upon these findings future research can build on to deepen and expand knowledge about the demographic transition.

Appendices

A. Definitions

Variable name	Description	Definition
Polity2	Combined polity score score	"The POLITY score is computed by subtracting the institutionalized autocracy score from the institutionalized democracy score; the resulting unified polity scale ranges from +10 (strongly democratic) to – 10 (strongly autocratic)." (PolityIV Manual, p.16)
Democracy	Polity IV democracy scorescore	"Institutionalized Democracy: Democracy is conceived as three essential, interdependent elements. One is the presence of institutions and procedures through which citizens can express effective preferences about alternative policies and leaders. Second is the existence of institutionalized constraints on the exercise of power by the executive. Third is the guarantee of civil liberties to all citizens in their daily lives and in acts of political participation." (Polity IV User's manual, p.14)
Polity2democ	Binary polity score	0 if polity2<6 1 if Polity2≥6
Lifeexpect	Life expectancy	"Life expectancy at birth indicates the number of years a newborn infant would live if prevailing patterns of mortality at the time of its birth were to stay the same throughout its life." (http://data.worldbank.org/indicator/SP.DYN.LE00.IN)
crbirthrate	Crude birth rates	"Crude birth rate indicates the number of live births occurring during the year, per 1,000 population estimated at midyear. Subtracting the crude death rate from the crude birth rate provides the rate of natural increase, which is equal to the rate of population change in the absence of migration." (http://data.worldbank.org/indicator/SP.DYN.CBRT.IN)
demotran	Demographic transition	0 if lifeexpect<50 or crbirthrates > 30 1 if lifeexpect>50 and crbirthrate<30
reher	Demographic transition according to Reher	Date of onset of fertility decline (Source: Reher, 2004)
yearssincedemotran	Years since demographic transition	Year-(reher)

Primschoolenroll	Primary school enrollment	"Gross enrollment ratio is the ratio of total enrollment, regardless of age, to the population of the age group that officially corresponds to the level of education shown. Primary education provides children with basic reading, writing, and mathematics skills along with an elementary understanding of such subjects as history, geography, natural science, social science, art, and music." (http://data.worldbank.org/indicator/SE.PRM.ENRR)
Secondschoolenroll	Secondary school enrollment	"Gross enrollment ratio is the ratio of total enrollment, regardless of age, to the population of the age group that officially corresponds to the level of education shown. Secondary education completes the provision of basic education that began at the primary level, and aims at laying the foundations for lifelong learning and human development, by offering more subject- or skill-oriented instruction using more specialized teachers." (http://data.worldbank.org/indicator/SE.SEC.ENRR)
school	Average years of schooling	Average Years of Schooling Attained (http://www.barrolee.com/)
Gdppc	GDP per capita	"GDP per capita is gross domestic product divided by midyear population. GDP is the sum of gross value added by all resident producers in the economy plus any product taxes and minus any subsidies not included in the value of the products. It is calculated without making deductions for depreciation of fabricated assets or for depletion and degradation of natural resources. Data are in current U.S. dollars." (http://data.worldbank.org/indicator/NY.GDP.PCAP.CD)
urbanpop	Urban population	"Urban population refers to people living in urban areas as defined by national statistical offices. It is calculated using World Bank population estimates and urban ratios from the United Nations World Urbanization Prospects." (http://data.worldbank.org/indicator/SP.URB.TOTL)
laboftotfem	Female labor participation rate (% of female population)	"Labor force participation rate is the proportion of the population ages 15 and older that is economically active: all people who supply labor for the production of goods and services during a specified period." (http://data.worldbank.org/indicator/SL.TLF.CACT.FE.ZS)
Demotrangdp	Demographic transition * GDP per capita	Interaction term between demotran and GDP per capita
ysdtgdppc	Years since demographic transition * GDP per capita	Interactions term between yearssince demotran and GDP per capita

B. Description of data

1. The demographic transition

a) List of demographic transition according to Reher

Group	Countries (Onset of fertility decline)
Forerunners (before 1935)	Argentina (1910) Austria (1915) Belgium (1905) Bulgaria (1925) Canada (1915) Cuba (1920) Denmark (1910) England and Wales (1910) Finland (1915) France (1900) Germany (1900) Hungary (1890) Italy (1925) Jamaica (1925) Netherlands (1910) Norway (1905) Portugal (1925) Romania (1935) Scotland (1905) Spain (1910) Sweden (1865) Switzerland (1910) United States (1925) Uruguay (1890)
Followers (1950-1964)	Antigua (1960) Barbados (1955) Brunei (1960) Chile (1960) India (1960) Israel (1955) Japan (1950) Korea (1960) Martinique (1960) Mauritius (1960) Phillipines (1955) Puerto Rico (1950) Qatar (1955) Reunion (1955) Singapore (1955) Sri Lanka (1960) Taiwan (1955)

Trailers (1965-1979)	Albania (1965) Algeria (1975) Armenia (1965) Azerbaijan (1965) Bahrain (1970) Belize (1965) Bermuda (1965) Bolivia (1975) Botswana (1975) Brazil (1965) Cayman Islands (1965) China (1970) Colombia (1965) Costa Rica (1965) Dominican Republic (1965) Ecuador (1970) Egypt (1965) El Salvador (1965) Georgia (1965) Guyana (1965) Indonesia (1970) Iraq (1975) Jordan (1975) Korea (People's Republic) (1970) Kuwait (1975) Kyrgyzstan (1965) Lebanon (1965) Malaysia (1965) Mexico (1970) Mongolia (1975) Morocco (1965) Myanmar (1975) Panama (1970) Peru (1975) Seychelles (1965) South Africa (1975) Surinam (1965) Swaziland (1975) Tanzania (1975) Thailand (1965) Trinidad and Tobago (1965) Tunisia (1965) Turkmenistan (1965) Uzbekistan (1965) Venezuela (1965) Western Sahara (1975) Zimbabwe (1970)

Latecomers (after 1980)	Afghanistan (2000) Angola (1995) Bangladesh (1980) Benin (1985) Bhutan (1995) Burkina Faso (2000) Burundi (1995) Cambodia (1990) Cameroon (1985) Central Africa (1990) Chad (2000) Comoros (1990) Congo (Dem. Republic) (2000) Congo (2000) Djibouti (1985) Eritrea (1990) Ethiopia (1990) Gabon (2000) Gambia (1985) Ghana (1985) Guatemala (1985) Guinea (1995) Guinea Bissau (2000) Haiti (1985) Honduras (1985) Iran (1985) Ivory Coast (1985) Kenya (1980) Lao People's Republic (1995) Lesotho (1985) Liberia (1995) Libya (1980) Madagascar (1990) Malawi (1980) Mali (1995) Mauritania (1980) Mozambique (2000) Namibia (1990) Nepal (1995) Nicaragua (1985) Niger (1985) Nigeria (1995) Oman (1995) Paraguay (1985) Rwanda (1995) Saudi Arabia (1980) Senegal (1980) Sierra Leone (2000) Somalia (2000) Sudan (1980) Syria (1985) Togo (1995) Uganda (2000) Vietnam (1980) Yemen (2000) Zambia (1980)

b) List of demographic transitions according to WDI data

Year of demographic transition	Country name
before 1960	Argentina Australia Austria Belarus Belgium Bermuda Canada Channel Croatia Cyprus Czech Rep Estonia Finland Georgia Germany Greece Hungary Isle Israel Italy Japan Liechtenstein Lithuania Latvia Moldavia Malta Montenegro North America Norway Poland Russian Slovenia Slovak Re Ukraine Uruguay United States
1962	Barbados
1963	Macedonia
1964	Armenia
1964	Bosnia and Herzegovina
1965	Bahamas
1965	Hongkong
1965	Kazakhstan
1966	Puerto Rico

1967	Trinidad and Tobago
1968	Grenada
1970	Azerbaijan
1970	Chile
1970	Cuba
1972	China
1972	Korea
1974	Virgin Islands (U.S.)
1975	Albania
1976	United Arab Emirates
1976	Guam
1976	New Caledonia
1977	Jamaica
1980	Guyana
1980	Panama
1982	St. Vincent and the Grenadines
1984	Brazil
1984	Colombia
1984	Costa Rica
1985	St. Lucia
1985	Qatar
1986	Mexico
1986	Turkey
1987	French Polynesia
1988	Fiji
1988	Tunisia
1988	Tunisia
1989	Bahrain
1989	Ecuador
1989	Kosovo
1990	Dominican Rep
1990	Kyrgyz Republic
1990	Peru
1991	India
1992	Egypt
1992	Iran
1994	Turkmenistan
1994	Uzbekistan
1995	Oman
1996	Maldives
1997	Bangladesh
1997	Saudi Arabia
1997	Syria
1998	Nicaragua
2001	Micronesia, Fed. Sts.
2001	Jordan
2001	Laos
2002	Gabon
2002	Pakistan

2003	Bolivia
2003	Namibia
2003	Samoa
2005	Botswana
2006	Djibouti
2009	Vanuatu
after 2010	Aruba
	Afghanistan
	Angola
	Algeria
	Benin
	Burkina Faso
	Belize
	Cote d'Ivoire
	Congo, Rep.
	Comoros
	Cape Verde
	Eritrea
	Ethiopia
	Ghana
	Gambia
	Guinea Bissau
	Equatorial Guinea
	Iraq
	Kenya
	Liberia
	Mauritius
	Malawi
	Mali
	Mozambique
	Mayotte
	Namibia
	Nicaragua
	Oman
	Pakistan
	Papua New Guinea
	Rwanda
	Senegal
	Somalia
	Sao Tome and Principe
	Suriname
	Swaziland
	Timor-Leste
	Tonga
	Uganda
	Vanuatu
	Yemen
	Zambia
	Zimbabwe

Date of demographic transition: Year in which life expectancies turn above 50 and crude birth rates fall below 30

Democratization waves according to Huntington

Wave	Countries
First wave	Australia
(1828-1926)	Canada
	Chile
	Finland
	Iceland
	Ireland
	New Zealand
	Sweden
	Switzerland
	United Kingdom
	United States

First reverse wave	Argentina
(1922-1942)	Austria
	Belgium
	Colombia
	Czechoslovakia
	Denmark
	Estonia
	France
	Greece
	Hungary
	Italy
	Japan
	Latvia
	Lithonia
	Netherlands
	Norway
	Poland
	Portugal
	Spain
	Uruguay
	West Germany
Second wave	Botswana
(1943-1962)	Costa Rica
	Gambia
	Israel
	Jamaica
	Malaysia
	Malta
	Sri Lanka
	Trinidad and Tobago
	Venezuela
Second reverse wave	--------------
(1958-1975)	Bolivia
	Burma
	Brazil
	Ecuador

	Fiji Ghana Guyana India Indonesia Lebanon Nigeria South Korea Pakistan Peru Philippines Turkey
Third wave (1974-)	Bulgaria Dominican Republic El Salvador Guatemala Haiti Honduras Mongolia Namibia Nicaragua Panama Papua New Guinea Romania Senegal Sudan Suriname

C. Data summaries

Data on demography

Variable	Obs	Mean	Std. Dev.	Min	Max
Lifeexpect	6789	61.995	12.350	23	82.99
Crbirthrate	6615	29.784	12.959	6.9	57.84
Demotran	6432	0.495	0.500	0	1
Yearssincedt	15878	-17.48	57.04	-200	146

Data on democracy

Variable	Obs	Mean	Std. Dev.	Min	Max
Democracy	15483	3.356	3.81	0	10
Polity2	15801	-0.923	7.005	-10	10

Other variables

Variable	Obs	Mean	Std. Dev.	Min	Max
primschoolenroll	3557	96.231	24.9	2.659	221.114
secondschoolenroll	3128	61.653	32.602	0	166.171
School	1623	3.985	3.257	0.04	12.25
Urbanpop	7574	50.137	24.956	2.04	100
laoftotfem	3608	47.741	15.817	9.5	86.8
gdppc	5273	5959.692	12013.62	35.368	186242.9

Interdependence between demographic transition and democracy

- Summary of democracy if demotran==0

Variable	Obs	Mean	Std. Dev.	Min	Max
Democracy	1550	2.571	3.442	0	10

- Summary of democracy if demotran==1

Variable	Obs	Mean	Std. Dev.	Min	Max
Democracy	1550	6.011	4.177	0	10

Development of average democracy scores and the average demographic transition over the past forty years (using 5-year average values of democracy scores and the demographic transition)

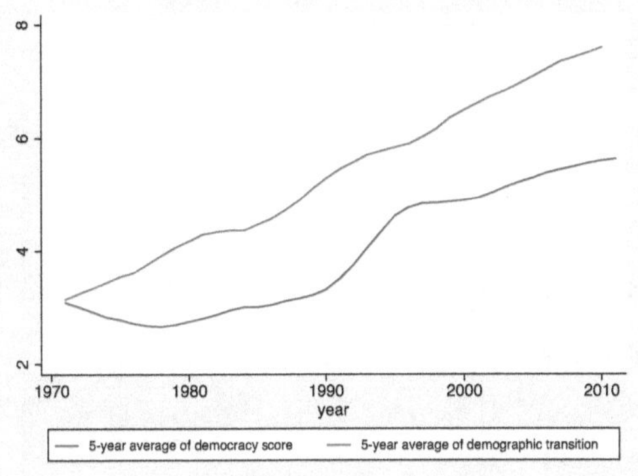

Figure 6 5-year average values of democracy scores and the demographic transition

D. Regression results[66]

1. OLS

OLS model with binary independent variable (demotran)[67]

Dependent variable	Polity2	Polity2	democracy	democracy	democracy	democracy	democracy	democracy	democracy	democracy	Polity2democ (binary)
	OLS	OLS	OLS	OLS	OLS (5- year-intervals)[68]	OLS (10- year-intervals)[69]	OLS Cross-sectional (year 2010)	OLS	OLS	OLS	Probit
Standard errors	HR	HR	HR	HR	HR	HR	HR	HR	HR	HR	HR
Demotran	1.19 (0.49)**	-1.7 (1.5)	0.84 (0.25)***	.568 (0.272)**	.869 (0.64)	1.47 (0.95)*	1.47 (0.95)*	.500 (0.33)		-1.12 (0.3)	-.14
L10	1.14 (0.64)**	1.5 (0.41)***	2.83 (0.28)***	.842 (0.35)**	.551 (0.84)	.282 (1.3)	.282 (1.3)	.356 (0.388)		0.11 (0.34)	.522***
L20	4.66 (0.53)***	0.9 (0.01)***	0.71 (0.33)***	2.285 (0.3)***	2.37 (0.75)**	1.2 (2.65)**	1.2 (2.65)**	2.51 (0.35)***	1.24** (0.51)	0.77 (0.31)**	.35**
Controls		Gdppc (L10,L20), urbanpop (L10, L20), schoolenrollpri (L10,L20) Polity2 (L10,L20)		gdppc	gdppc	gdppc	gdppc	Gdppc, primschoolenroll	L20.secondaryedu, l20.lgdppc, l20.urbanpop	Gdppc (L10,L20) schoolenrollmentprimarygross (L10,L20) Urbanpop (L10,L20) Democracy (l10,L20)	Gdppc (L10,L20), urbanpop (L10, L20), schoolenrollpri (L10,L20)
n	2034	787	2015	1871	362	172	172	1600	496	771	1060
Adjusted R^2	0.18	0.647	0.22	0.28	0.29	0.32	0.32	0.33	0.3	0.65	

[66] In parentheses, t-statistics based on HR and HAC standard errors respectively. ***,**,* denote 1%, 5% and 10% significance levels respectively. If not denoted differently the whole sample is used.

[67] The regressions are executed using only the 10th and 20th lag of the demographic transition as additional regressors as well as using all 20 lags [l(1/20)demotran] as regressors which both yield similar results. Therefore only the 10th and 20th lag are reported. Detailed information can be found in the do-file (available upon request).

[68] The sample is split up into 5-year-intervals and the value for each fifth year is the average value of the previous five years.

[69] The sample is split up into 10-year-intervals and the value for each tenth year is the average value of the previous ten years.

OLS model with continuous independent variable (years since demographic transition)

Dependent variable	democracy	democracy	democracy	democracy	democracy	democracy	democracy	democracy
	OLS	OLS	OLS	OLS	OLS	OLS	OLS	Ordered probit
Standard Errors	HR	HR	HR	HR	HR	HR	HR	HR
Time period	1960-2010	1960-2010	1960-2010 (5-year-intervals)	1960-2010 (10-year-intervals)	1960	1980	2010	1960-2010
Yearssincedt	0.06 (0.003)***	.0257 (0.014)**	.065 (0.007)***	0.06 (0.01)***	.108 (0.019)***	0.066 (0.03)**	0.062 (0.01)***	.0258(.0013)***
Controls	lgdppc	Lgdppc, school, urbanpop, laboftotfem	lgdppc	lgdppc	lgdppc	lgdppc	lgdppc	lgdppc
n	2456	200	641	276	26	47	51	2456
Adjusted R^2	0.38	0.44	0.33	0.36	0.43	0.28	0.2	

Binary independent variable

Dependent variable	Polity2	democracy	democracy	democracy	democracy	democracy	Polity2	democracy	democracy
Time/Country FE?	Country FE	Country FE	Country FE 5-year-intervals	Country FE	Country FE	Country FE 5-year-intervals	Country FE	Country FE	Country FE
Standard errors	HAC	HAC	HAC	HAC	HAC	HAC	HAC	HAC	HAC
Demotran (Demographic transition)	.89 (1.3)	0.22 (0.39)	.40 (0.43)	0.03 (0.44)	.316 (.64)	-.144 (0.5)	-3.0 (0.9)	-1.8 (0.5)	-1.7 (0.5)
L10	1.4 (1.0)*	0.78* (0.56)	.8000(0.66)	0.37 (0.65)	.898 (1.05)	.436 (0.82)	-0.7 (1.0)	0.43 (0.64)	-0.4 (0.7)
L20	2.61 (1.4)**	1.32** (0.76)	2.223 (1.02)**	0.82 (0.78)	3.6 (1.6)**	1.83 (1.1)*	0.65 (1.2)	0.27 (0.68)	-0.08 (0.7)
LnLifeexpect (Life expectancy)							11.0 (4.3)**	5.63 (2.6)**	5.8 (2.9)**
L10							6.0 (3.0)*	4.8 (2.0)**	5.4(2.3)**
L20							13.7 (6.3)**	4.9 (3.3)*	7.1 (4.0)**
Lncrbirthrate							-3.9 (2.9)	-2.2 (1.6)	-1.3 (1.7)
L10							-0.7 (1.9)	-1.0 (1.1)	-0.8 (1.7)
L20							2.2 (1.3)	1.1 (0.7)	-2.0(1.1)**
Controls				Lgdppc, l10.lgdppc, l20.lgdppc	Lgdppc, l10.lgdppc, l20.lgdppc, school, l10.school, l20.school	Lgdppc, l10.lgdppc, l20.lgdppc			Lgdppc, l10.lgdppc, l20.lgdppc
n	2034 (75 countries)	2015 (75 countries)	378 (72 countries)	1871 (71 countries)	182 (47 countries)	276 (59 countries)	2034 (75 countries)	2015 (75 countries)	1424 (63 countries)
Adjusted R^2	0.049	.04	0.07	.1	0.23	0.12	0.23	0.2	.2

Continuous independent variable

Dependent variable	democracy	democracy	democracy	democracy	democracy
Time/Country FE?	Country FE	Country FE	Country FE	Country FE	Country FE 5-year intervals
Standard errors	HAC	HAC	HAC	HAC	HAC
Yearssincedt (Reher specification)	0.1 (0.02)***	.102 (0.042)**			.562 (.010)***
Yearssincedemotran (WDI specification)			.075 (0.03)**	.082 (0.09)	
Controls	lgppc	Lgdppc, school	Lgdppc	Lgdppc, school	gdppc
n	2456 (60 countries)	330 (42 countries)	184 (23 countries)	1468 (35 countries)	983 (142 countries)
Adjusted R^2	0.2	0.15	0.15	0.14	.74

Binary independent variable

Dependent variable	Polity2	democracy	democracy	democracy	democracy	Polity2	democracy
Time/Country FE?	Country FE, year FE	Country FE, year FE	Country FE, year FE	Country FE, year FE	Country FE, year FE 5-year intervals	Country FE, year FE	Country FE, year FE
Standard errors	HAC	HAC	HAC	HAC	HAC	HAC	HAC
Demotran (Demographic transition)	-1.9 (0.83)**	-1.2 (0.49)*	-1.14 (0.5)**	-1.1 (0.5)*	-1.0065 (0.51)	-2.5 (0.9)**	-1.62 (0.53)
L10	-0.29 (0.9)	-0.07 (0.6)	-.103 (0.64)	0.02 (0.7)	-.095 (0.68)	-0.1 (1.0)	-0.18 (6.4)
L20	0.09 (1.3)	0.06 (0.7)	.265 (0.7)	0.13 (0.8)	.898 (1.00)	1.3 (1.2)	0.52 (0.66)
LnLifeexpect (Life expectancy)						8.8 (4.3)**	4.6 (2.4)**
L10						4.1 (3.9)	3.8 (2.3)*
L20						1.7 (6.8)	-0.06 (3.9)
Lncrbirthrate						-0.8 (2.9)	-1.05 (1.6)
L10						1.1 (2.0)	-0.3 (1.2)
L20						5.4 (1.6)	2.3 (0.9)**
Controls			Lgdppc	Lgdppc, l10.lgdppc, l20.lgdppc			
n	2034 (75 countries)	2015 (75 countries)	1871 (71 countries)	1424 (63 countries)	378 (72 countries)	1980 (73 countries)	1961 (73 countries)
Adjusted R^2	0.26	0.2	.185	0.2	0.21	0.28	0.23

Continuous independent variable

Dependent variable	democracy	democracy	democracy	democracy
Time/Country FE?	Country FE, Time FE	Country FE, Time FE	Country FE, Time FE 5-year-intervals	Country FE, Time FE
Standard errors	HAC	HAC	HAC	HAC
yearssincedt	0.02 (0.006)***	0.06 (0.02)**	.063 (0.028)**	.084 (.039)**
Controls		lgdppc	lgdppc	Lgdppc, school
n	12895 (135 countries)	2456 (60 countries)	641(60 countries)	330 (42 countries)
Adjusted R^2	0.3	0.23	0.2	0.17

4. Interactions with income

Group	Full sample	Full sample	Full sample	Only rich countries (if gdppc>6000)	Only poor countries (if gdppc<6000)
Dependent variable	democracy	democracy	democracy	democracy	democracy
	Country FE	Country FE	Country FE	Country FE	Country FE
Standard Errors	HAC	HAC	HAC	HAC	HAC
Yearssincedt	.10 (0.02)***		.1 (0.02)***	.0092 (.007)	.112 (.021)***
Yearssincedt*gdppc	-.0000521 (.0000259)**				
demotran		1.33(0.48)***			
Demotran*gdppc		-.0000893 (.0000412)**			
gdppc		.000119 (.0000465) **			
Controls	lgdppc		lgdppc	lgdppc	lgdppc
n	2456 (60 countries)	2767 (73 countries)	2456 (60 countries)	444 (20 countries)	2012 (60 countries)
Adjusted R^2	0.22	0.04	0.2	0.01	0.22

5. Time of demographic transition

Dependent variable	democracy	democracy	democracy	democracy
Group	Full sample	Forerunner (before 1935)	Followers & Trailers (1950-1979)	Latecommer (after 1980)
Standard Errors	Country FE HAC	Country FE HAC	Country FE HAC	Country FE HAC
Yearssincedt	.1 (0.02)***	.0112 (0.053)	.086 (0.0339)**	.1239 (.031)***
Controls	lgdppc	lgdppc	lgdppc	lgdppc
n	2456 (60 countries)	533 (12 countries)	1033 (24 countries)	708 (20 countries)
Adjusted R^2	0.2	0.09	0.22	0.25

6. Effect of life expectancies and crude birth rates

Dependent variable	Polity2	democracy	Polity2	democracy	democracy	Polity2	democracy	democracy
Model	OLS	OLS	Country FE	Country FE	Country FE	Country FE, year FE	Country FE, year FE	Country FE, year FE
Standard errors	HR	HR	HAC	HAC	HAC	HAC	HAC	HAC
Lnlifeexpect								
L10	6.42 (0.9)***	4.26 (0.46)***	16.9 (4.4)***	7.77 (2.2)***	7.7 (2.4)***	3.3(4.8)	1.75 (2.9)	6.12 (3.5)**
lncrbirthrate								
L10	-5.3 (0.4)***	-3.1 (0.2)***	-3.2 (1.9)*	-1.9 (1.0)*	-.88 (0.9)	2.5 (1.7)	0.7 (1.0)	-0.16 (1.6)
Controls					L10.lgdppc			L10.school l10.lgdppcn
n	2770	2742	2696	2669 (75 countries)	2461 (73 countries)	2696 (75 countries)	2669 (75 countries)	391 (62 countries)
Adjusted R^2	0.24	0.28	0.19	0.16	0.17	0.27	0.21	0.22

7. Channel analysis

Correlation matrix

	democracy	yearssincedt	school	gdppc	crbirthrate	lifeexpect	urbanpop
democracy	1						
yearssincedt	0.6220	1					
school	0.6482	0.8405	1				
gdppc	0.5016	0.5827	0.6673	1			
crbirthrate	-0.5521	-0.8200	-0.7997	-0.6152	1		
lifeexpect	0.5105	0.7257	0.7595	0.5572	-0.8752	1	
urbanpop	0.4303	0.5751	0.6244	0.4745	-0.7162	0.7929	1

Effect of channels

Dependent variable	school	Urbanpop	laboftotfem	gdppc	democracy
	Country FE	Country FE	Country FE	Country FE	OLS
yearssincedt	.0663(.00695)***	.521 (0.0423)***	.2324 (.0376)***	201.8 (43.4)***	-
school	-	.029 (0.085)	-	-39.93 (93.9)	.629 (0.1)***
urbanpop	-	-	-	-	.0217 (0.0134)*
laboftotfem	-	-	-	-	.01124 (.01473)
gdppc	-8.36e-06(.0000196)	-.00025 (.000069)***	.000074 (.0000334)**	-	.0000915 (.0000318)**
n	476 (75 countries)	476 (75 countries)	2058 (82 countries)	476 (75 countries)	229
Adjusted R^2	0.13	0.7	0.4	0.23	0.42

Summary of effects

Channel	Effect of demographic transition on channel	Effect of channel on democracy	Effect of demographic transition on democracy
Education (school)	.0663(.00695)***	.629 (0.1)***	0.0417
Urbanization (urbanpop)	.521 (0.0423)***	.0217 (0.0134)*	0.0113
Female laborforce participation(laboftotfem)	.2324 (.0376)***	.01124 (.01473)	0.00261
GDP (gdppc)	201.8 (43.4)***	.0000915 (.0000318)**	0.0185
Total effect			0.074

Bibliography

Acemoglu, D., S. Johnson, J. A. Robinson, and P. Yared. "Income and Democracy." *American Economic Review* 98.3 (2008): 808-42.

Acemoglu, D., and J. A Robinson. "Economic Origins of Dictatorship and Democracy." *Journal of Economics* 92.3 (2007): 293-95.

Acemoglu, D., and S. Johnson. "Disease and Development: The Effect of Life Expectancy on Economic Growth." *Journal of Political Economy* 115.6 (2007): 925-85.

Acemoglu, D., S. Johnson, J. A. Robinson, and Pierre Yared. "From Education to Democracy?" *American Economic Review* 95.2 (2005): 44-49.

Adams, P., Hurd, M. D., McFadden, D., Merrill, A. and Ribeiroa, T. „Healthy, wealthy, and wise? Tests for direct causal paths between health and socioeconomic status." *Journal of Econometrics* 112 (2003): 3-56.

Amin, S., and N. Thrift. *The Emancipatory City?*. L. Lees (ed.). London: Sage, 2004.

Banks, A. "Cross-National Time-Series Data Archive 1815-2007". http://hdl.handle.net/1902.1/11448 Databanks International [Distributor] V1 [Version]. Accessed: March 1st, 2012.

Barro, R. J. and J. Lee. "Barro-Lee Educational Attainment Dataset 1950-2010", 2011. http://www.barrolee.com/data/full1.htm. Accessed: February 12th, 2012.

Barro, R. J. "Determinants of Democracy." *Journal of Political Economy* 107.6 (1999): 158-183.

---. "Democracy and Growth." *Journal of Economic Growth* 1.1 (1996): 1-27.

Bar, M. and O. Leukhina. "The role of adult mortality in the transmission of knowledge." *Journal of Economic Growth* 15.4 (2011): 291–321.

Baum, M. A., and D. A. Lake. "The Political Economy of Growth: Democracy and Human Capital." *American Journal of Political Science* 47.2 (2003): 333-47.

Bhrolcháin, M. Ní, and T. Dyson. "On Causation in Demography: Issues and Illustrations." *Population and Development Review* 33.1 (2007): 1-36.

Bloom, D., D. Canning and J. Sevilla. *Economic Growth and the Demographic Transition*. Working Paper 8685. National Bureau of Economic Research, December 2001. http://www.nber.org/papers/w8685. Accessed: February 15th, 2012.

Bloom, D. E., D. Canning, G. Fink, and J. E. Finlay. "Fertility, Female Labor Force Participation, and the Demographic Dividend." *Journal of Economic Growth*, 14.2 (2009): 79-101.

Bollen, K. A. and R. W. Jackman. „Democracy, Stability, and Dichotomies". *American Sociological Review* 54. 4 (1989): 612-621.

Canning, D. "The Causes and Consequences of Demographic Transition." *Population Studies* (2011): 1-9.

---. "Progress in Health around the World." *Human Development Research Papers.* HDRP-2010-43, Human Development Report Office (HDRO): United Nations Development Programme (UNDP), 2010.

Chesnais, J.-C. *The demographic transition: Stages, patterns and economic implications, a longitudinal study of sixty-seven countries covering the period 1720–1984.* Oxford: Clarendon Press, 1992.

Cervelatti, M. and U. Sunde. *Democratization, Violent Social Conflicts, and Growth.* IZA DP No. 5643, 2011.

Cervellati, M. and U. Sunde. "Life Expectancy and Economic Growth: The Role of the Demographic Transition." *Journal of Economic Growth* 16 (2011): 99-133.

Cervelatti, M. and U. Sunde. *Human Capital, Mortality and Fertility: A Unified Theory of the Economic and Demographic Transition.* IZA DP No. 2905, 2007.

Cincotta, R. P. "Half a Chance: Youth Bulges and Transitions to Liberal Democracy," *Environmental Change and Security Project Report* 13 (2008): 10-18.

---. "Does a Demographic Transition Promote a Democratic Transition?" *Proc. of Annual Meeting of the American Political Science Association.* 2007.

---. "Demographic Security Comes of Age." *Environmental Change and Security Project Report* 10 (2004): 24-29.

Coale, A. J. "The decline of fertility in Europe since the eighteenth century as a chapter in human demographic history". *The Decline of Fertility in Europe.* Ed. A. J. Coale and S. C. Watkins. Princeton: Princeton University Press,1986. 1–30.

---. "The demographic transition" *International Population Conference vol. 1.* Liège: IUSSP, 1973. 53–72.

Collier, P. "Doing well out of war: An economic perspective." *Greed and Grievance: Economic Agendas in Civil Wars.* Ed. Berdal, M. and D. Malone. Boulder, CO: Lynne Rienner, 2000.

Cranmer, S. J., and R. M. Siverson. "Demography, Democracy and Disputes: The Search for the Elusive Relationship Between Population Growth and International Conflict." *The Journal of Politics* 70.03 (2008): 794-806.

Cutler, D., A. Deaton and A. Lleras-Muney. "The Detterminants of Mortality." *The Journal of Economic Perspectives,* 20.3 (2006): 97-120.

Glaeser, E., G. Ponzetto and A. Shleifer . "Why Does Democracy Need Education?" *Journal of Economic Growth* 12.2 (2007): 77-99.

Dahan, M. and D. Tsiddon. "Demographic Transition, Income Distribution, and Economic Growth." *Journal of Economic Growth* 3 (1998): 29-52.

Desai, R., A. Olofsgård and T. M. Yousef. "The Logic of Authoritarian Bargains." *Economics&Politics* 21.1 (2009): 93-125.

de Vries, J. "Problems in the measurement, description, and analysis of historical urbanization" *Urbanization in History*. Ed. A. van der Woude, A. Hayami, and J. de Vries. Oxford: Clarendon Press, 1990.

Dewey, J. *Democracy and Education. An introduction to the philosophy of education.* New York: Free Press, 1916.

Dyson, T. "The Role of the Demographic Transition in the Process of Urbanization." *Population and Development Review* 37 (2011): 34-54.

---. *Population and Development: The Demographic Transition.* London: Zed Books, 2010.

---. "A Partial Theory of World Development: The Neglected Role of the Demographic Transition in the Shaping of Modern Society." *International Journal of Population Geography* 7.2 (2001): 67-90.

Franco, A., C. Alvarez-Dardet, and M. T. Ruiz. "Effect of democracy on health: ecological study". *British Medical Journal* 329 (2004): 1421-23.

Feng, Y. and P. J. Zak. „The Democratic Transition Process" *The Journal of Conflict Resolution* 43.2 (1999): 162-177.

Galor, O. *The Demographic Transition: Causes and Consequences.* Working Paper 17057. National Bureau of Economic Research. May 2011. http://www.nber.org/papers/w17057. Accessed: February 15th, 2012.

Goldstone, J., R. Bates, T. Gurr, M. Lustik, M. Marshall, J. Ulfelder, and M. Woodward. "A Global Forecasting Model of Political Instability." *Annual Meeting of the American Political Science*, 2005.

Goldstone, J. A. "Demography, Environment, and Security." *Environmental Conflict.* Ed. Paul F. Diehl and Nils Petter Gleditsch. Boulder: Westview, 2001.

---. *Revolution and Rebellion in the Early Modern World.* Berkeley: University of California Press, 1991.

Grebenik, E. "Demography, Democracy, and Demonology." *Population and Development Review* 15.1 (1989): 1-22.

Hayes, A. and L. Cai. "Using heteroskedasticity-consistent standard error estimators in OLS regression." *Behavior Research Methods.* 39.4 (2007): 709-722.

Hegre, H., C. Knutsen and E. Rod. *The Determinants of Democracy: A Sensitivity Analysis.* Working Paper. Centre for the Study of Civil War, 2012.

Hsiao, C. *Analysis of Panel Data.* Cambridge: University of Cambridge Press, 2003.

Huntington, Samuel P. *The Third Wave: Democratization in the Late 20th Century.*

Norman (Oklahoma): University of Oklahoma Press, 1991.

Laski, H. J. *Encyclopedia of the Social Sciences. Vol. V.* New York: Macmillan, 1937

Lipset, S. M. "Some Social Requisites of Democracy: Economic Development and Political Legitimacy." *The American Political Science Review* 53.1 (1959): 69-105.

Lorentzen, P., J. McMillan and R. Wacziarg. *Death and Development.* Working Paper No. 11620. National Bureau of Economic Research, September 2005. http://www.nber.org/papers/w11620. Accessed: February 15th, 2012.

Marshall, M. "Polity IV Project. Dataset User's Manual". 2011. Centre for Systematic Peace. www.systemicpeace.org/polity/polity4.htm. Accessed: February 10th, 2012.

Mumford, L. *The Culture of Cities.* Ed. P. Kasinitz. New York: New York University Press, 1995.

Murtin, F. and R. Wacziarg. *The Democratic Transition.* Working Paper No. 17432. National Bureau of Economic Research, September 2011. http://www.nber.org/papers/w17432. Accessed: March 8th 2012.

Navia, P. and T. D. Zweifel. "Democracy, Dictatorship, and Infant Mortality Revisited." *Journal of Democracy* 14.3 (2003): 90-103.

Papaioannou, E. and G. Siourounis. 2006. "Economic and Social Factors Driving the Third Wave of Democratization." *Journal of Comparative Economics* 36 (2008): 365-387.

Reher, D. S. "Economic and Social Implications of the Demographic Transition." *Population and Development Review* 37 (2011): 11-33.

---. "The Demographic Transition Revisited as a Global Process." *Population, Space and Place* 10.1 (2004): 19-41.

Rodgers, D. *Separate but Equal Democratization?* Working Paper No. 2011/16. UNU-Wider. World Institute for Development Economics Research. March 2011.

Rueschemeyer, D., E.H. Stephens and J.D. Stephens. *Capitalist Development and Democracy.* Chicago: University of Chicago Press, 1992.

Shentu, Y. and M. Xi. "A note on dichotomization in the presence of contamination and model misspecification". *Statistics in Medicine* 29.21 (2010): 2200-14.

Smith, J. P. *Consequences and Predictors of New Health Events.* NBER Working Paper No.10063. 2003.

Stock, J. and M. Watson. *Introduction to Econometrics.* Boston: Pearson/Addison Wesley, 2007.

Sunde, U. *Wirtschaftliche Entwicklung und Demokratie: ist Demokratie ein Wohlstandsmototr ode rein Wohlstandsprodukt?* IZA DP No.2244, 2006.

Tavares, J. and R. Wacziarg. "How democracy affects growth". *European Economic Review* 45 (2001): 1341-78.

Torre, R. and M. Myrskylä. "Income inequality and population health: a panel data analysis on 21 developed countries (Working Paper 2011-006)" Max Planck Institute for Demographic Research. February 2011. http://www.demogr.mpg.de. Accessed: March 25th, 2012.

Urdal, H. "A Clash of Generations? Youth Bulges and Political Violence." *International Studies Quarterly* 50.3 (2006): 607-29.

Waylan, G. "Conceptualizing Gender Relations in Transition Politics." *World Politics* 46.3 (1994): 327-54.

Weber, M. *General Economic History*. Glencoe: The Free Press, 1950.

---. *Essays in Sociology*. New York: Oxford University Press, 1946.

Woods, R. "Urban-rural mortality differentials: An unresolved debate" *Population and Development Review* 29.1 (2003): 29–46.

World Bank. "World Development Indicator Database". http://data.worldbank.org/data-catalog/world-development-indicators. Accessed: February 2nd, 2012.

Zellner, A. and H. Theil. "Three-Stage Least Squares: Simultaneous estimation of simultaneous equations." *Econometrica* 30.1 (1962): 54-78.

www.ingramcontent.com/pod-product-compliance
Lightning Source LLC
LaVergne TN
LVHW102228300926
849160LV00005B/67

* 9 7 8 3 9 5 4 8 9 2 5 8 7 *